nory of a great Dancer

ANNA PAVLOVA
TWENTIETH CENTURY
BALLERINA

ANNA PAVLOVA
TWENTIETH CENTURY
BALLERINA

JANE PRITCHARD
WITH CAROLINE HAMILTON

Booth-Clibborn Editions

CONTENTS

It was Anna Pavlova, and no one else, who opened the world to ballet. It was she who did the back-breaking work of pioneering. It was Pavlova who found and cultivated audiences for contemporary ballet companies. Her service to ballet is priceless. No other single human being did more for ballet than she. To all the millions of people for whom she danced she brought a little of herself; she brought a little happiness to them all. Her genius was as intangible as the legacy she left behind. What remains of Pavlova today is not a movement in the art, not a tendency, not even a series of dances. It is something far less concrete, but possibly far more valuable: inspiration.

1929, Hilda Butsova
dancer with Pavlova 1912–1925,
Dance Magazine, November 1972

As Zulma in the ballet *Giselle* Act II, St Petersburg, 1899

IMPERIAL BALLERINA

Anna Pavlova was born on 31 January 1881. Details of her birth and the identity of her father remain uncertain but she appears to have been of mixed Jewish and Russian origin. Despite her fame, many details of Pavlova's personal life are shrouded in mystery, including the nature of her relationship with Victor Dandré, who is variously referred to as her husband, lover, protector, manager and collaborator. (It seems unlikely, given Dandré's different accounts of their wedding, that they were ever actually married.)

Pavlova grew up near St Petersburg with a love of the countryside but no obvious artistic interest, until, in 1890, she was taken by her mother to the Maryinsky Theatre to see Marius Petipa's masterpiece, *The Sleeping Beauty*, one of the first performances of the multi-act ballet to Piotr Tchaikovsky's score. Sitting in a cheap seat up in 'the gods', Pavlova was captivated and she determined not just to dance but to become a ballerina.

A year and a half later, in the autumn of 1891, at the age of ten Pavlova successfully entered the Imperial Ballet School. The School by this time was one of the finest, and the dancers' training included elements of the older French school and the new Italian style that emphasised virtuosity.

Throughout her career Pavlova preferred to disguise her technique. As Nicolas Legat, one of her partners (and later a teacher), commented, 'she captivated her audience by the amazing vivacity and expressiveness of her personality'.[1] Her dancing had a lightness missing from the work of many of her contemporaries and she used her arms and hands to add to this effect. But if she avoided the overt display of virtuosity characteristic of some of the Italian ballerinas, Pavlova certainly brought something of their dramatic quality to many of her roles.

Compared to many dancers of the period Pavlova was slightly built. In static photographs, for which poses had to be held for some time, it was hard for dancers to look featherweight and their training tended to compact muscles rather than lengthen them. Furthermore, the fashions of the day – the corseted torso, the cut of the tutus and hair piled on top of their heads – contributed to the dancers' weightier appearance. It is clear from photographs that Pavlova was slimmer than most of her contemporaries, and from relatively early in her career she dressed her hair closer to the head.

At the Imperial Ballet School students gained stage experience by taking part in student performances. On 29 March 1898, a year before her graduation, Pavlova attracted attention in a school performance of *The Two Stars* by Petipa. Seven months later, on 21 October, at a benefit performance for dancer and teacher Anna Johanson, she made her first featured appearance at the Maryinsky in the 'Pas des aimées' in *Pharaoh's Daughter*. On 11 April 1899 Pavlova appeared at her official graduation performing ballets that included Pavel Gerdt's *The Imaginary Dryads* and Alexander Gorsky's *Clorinda*.

By the time the new 1899–90 season opened in September Pavlova was a fully-fledged member of the company, appearing in distinctive roles. The first, on 26 September, was as Zulma, one of Myrtha's attendant 'wilis' (the vampire-like women who at night attempt to dance men to death) in Act II of *Giselle*. Within five months, on 7 February 1900, she created her first new role – as Hoarfrost in Petipa's *The Seasons*, to music by Alexander Glazounov.

At the start of the following season, on 10 September, Pavlova made her debut as Flora in the mythical ballet *The Awakening of Flora*. This was a role that had been created for the prima ballerina Mathilde Kschessinskaya, a very different dancer to Pavlova. Kschessinskaya had a clear, strong technique, emulating the Italian ballerinas who had come into fashion in St Petersburg around the time she graduated. Flora was therefore something of a challenge for Pavlova but, given that in 1914 she had a version of the ballet mounted for her own company, it was obviously one that she enjoyed. The role of Apollo, which was danced at Pavlova's first performance by her teacher Pavel Gerdt, was soon assumed by Mikhail Fokine, and the two danced together in many productions at the Imperial Ballet over the next decade.

Over the next few years Pavlova's repertoire expanded, allowing her to take on a wide range of roles. On 2 December 1901 she danced the role of Princess Florine, who appears in the challenging pas de deux with the Bluebird in the last act of Petipa's *The Sleeping Beauty*. Later the same month, on 19 December, she appeared as Lise in *The Magic Flute*. In this slight ballet Oberon, disguised as a hermit, gives Luc a flute which

makes everyone dance, enabling him to win Lise from her rich suitor and greedy mother. This ballet revealed Pavlova's talent for witty soubrette roles and an aptitude for comedy that was later seen in her appearances as Swanilda in *Coppélia* and Lise in *La Fille mal gardée*.

In 1902, the year in which she was promoted to the rank of second soloist, Pavlova performed the dramatic role of Nikiya, the betrayed oriental temple dancer of Petipa's 1877 ballet *La Bayadère*. It was a role that had been monopolised by prima ballerina assoluta Mathilde Kschessinskaya since Petipa's restaging of the ballet in 1900. When Kschessinskaya became pregnant, however, she agreed to coach Pavlova in the role. Pavlova also studied at this time with Eugenia Sokolova (who appears to have been important in helping Pavlova revitalise roles in established ballets). *La Bayadère* is set in a fantasy India, although Pavlova's adaptation of the costumes suggested a more faithful interpretation of orientalism than that of some of her colleagues. However, it was her dramatic interpretation of Nikiya's death having been bitten by the snake that surprised her audience: her improvised movements gave a deliberately distorted response to the score.

In 1903 Pavlova added two further works to her repertoire that she would perform throughout her career. The first, on 7 February, was *The Fairy Doll,* which was presented at the Hermitage Theatre, within the tsar's Winter Palace in St Petersburg. Pavlova actually created the role of the Spanish Doll (one of several 'Spanish' solos in which she excelled), although when she had the ballet mounted for her company by Ivan Clustine in 1914 she danced the title role. The first Russian version of *The Fairy Doll* was choreographed by the brothers Sergei and Nicolas Legat. Theirs was just one of dozens of productions inspired by and adapted from the popular Viennese ballet *Die Puppenfee* (1888), about dolls in a toyshop coming to life, choreographed by Joseph Hassreiter to music by Josef Bayer. The Legats' production of *The Fairy Doll* was one of the first ballets designed by Léon Bakst, who was to become one of the most influential designers of the early twentieth century and one of the few to receive acknowledgement in Pavlova's programmes.

Even more important was Pavlova's debut on 30 April at the Maryinsky in the title role of the betrayed village girl who loses her reason in *Giselle*. This was a role that she would continue to work on throughout her life, and it is evident that in her first performances she was finding her own way to interpret a part which, like Nikiya in *La Bayadère*, calls for both dramatic acting in the 'real' world and ethereality in the supernatural. The leading Russian critic Valentin Svetlov was increasingly impressed by Pavlova's performances: the way she lost her reason at the end of Act I, evident even in posed studio photographs showing her with dishevelled hair, wildly clutching Albrecht's discarded sword; and her convincing appearance as a 'wili' in the second scene, set in the forest by night, which revealed her 'ethereal, transparent, quivering dances'.[2] Giselle was to remain one of Pavlova's most important roles, one that never failed to grip her viewers.

At around this time Pavlova also began to dance at other Imperial Theatres: the Bolshoi in Moscow and Wielki in Warsaw. Like many other young ballerinas she went to Milan to study with

As Flore with Mikhail Fokine as Apollo in
The Awakening of Flora

Above:
Bakst's design for the Spanish
Doll in *The Fairy Doll,*
produced as a postcard sold
in aid of the Red Cross

Left:
As the Spanish Doll in
The Fairy Doll created
for the Hermitage Theatre

Catarina Beretta who appears to have had the ability to enhance not only dancers' techniques but also their stamina, a key attribute for the long and demanding roles in the Imperial Ballet's repertoire.

On 2 May 1904 Pavlova made her debut in *Paquita*, a ballet set in Spain after the Peninsular War. She took the title role as the beautiful orphan girl, and was partnered by Fokine as the handsome Lucien. It was a role that allowed her to exhibit both drama and comedy, and to present a range of dance styles culminating in the formal classicism of the closing 'grand pas classique', a solo which was newly choreographed for Pavlova by Petipa, to music added to the ballet by Riccardo Drigo. This 'grand pas' later became a useful showcase work in Pavlova's repertory; indeed, it was the very last ballet she danced at Golders Green Hippodrome in 1930.

The trajectory of Pavlova's early career must, of course, be seen in its historical context. By the middle of the first decade of the twentieth century Russia was in turmoil. The optimism that marked the two-hundredth anniversary celebrations of St Petersburg in May 1903 was short-lived and by the following year political tension had increased. By November 1904 there were nationwide demands for liberalisation of the press, and in December the tsar issued a manifesto promising limited reforms. This merely prompted strike action at the Putilov engineering works which in turn sparked off further strikes and led to the tragic events of 'Bloody Sunday' (when at least a thousand peaceful protestors were killed or injured by government troops in the centre of St Petersburg). The general unrest was exacerbated by the war with Japan that had begun on 8 February 1904 and culminated in the humiliating capture of Port Arthur and the destruction of the Russian fleet the following year.

Dancers from the Imperial Ballet were not impervious to these events. They took part in the strikes in the autumn, and the newly promoted ballerina, Anna Pavlova, became one of twelve delegates elected to discuss the improvement of conditions with the management. Requests included not only higher salaries and a five-day working week but also greater control over artistic matters, such as the right for dancers to choose the regisseurs who oversaw rehearsals, and the reinstatement of ballet master Marius Petipa, his assistant Alexander Shiryaev and teacher Alfred Bekefi. The general mood of protest, allied to a concern over falling standards, probably contributed to the desire by Russian dancers to look outside their home company and seek work in situations in which they had more control over their careers. It was around this time that Pavlova began studying privately for three years under the great teacher Enrico Cecchetti, whom she credited with improving the use of her back and hands.

Unlike some of her contemporaries, whose careers suffered as a result, Pavlova desisted from further revolutionary activity and continued to receive new roles. On 4 December 1905 she made her debut as the vivacious Kitri, the inn-keeper's daughter, in Alexander Gorsky's production of *Don Quixote*. A month and a half later, on 15 January 1906, she danced Bint-Anta in Gorsky's reworking of Petipa's *The Pharaoh's Daughter* at the Bolshoi in Moscow, and two weeks later essentially the same role – that of Aspicia – in Petipa's original ballet. Once again this broke Kschessinskaya's monopoly of the role.

The year 1907 was highly significant for Pavlova. Mikhail Fokine created a series of innovative ballets for her, culminating on 22 December with her first performance of *The Swan*. On 10 February Fokine created his first *Chopiniana*. For this he added to a suite arranged by Glazounov, Chopin's Waltz in C Sharp Minor (Op. 64. No. 2), which was used for a pas de deux in the style of mid-nineteenth century lithographs of the Romantic ballerina, Marie Taglioni. This was so admired that it became the starting point for the second *Chopiniana* on 8 March, in which Pavlova danced the pas de deux with Nijinsky (and the whole production evoked the acclaimed 1832 ballet *La Sylphide*). It was this *Chopiniana* which was to evolve into *Les Sylphides*, becoming an anchor-work of Serge Diaghilev's Ballets Russes. Pavlova always retained the original waltz and her own variant of *Chopiniana* in her repertory.

Pavlova's private class with Enrico Cecchetti in her St Petersburg studio apartment. Steinberg's portrait of the dancer, *Pavlova as Muse*, hangs on the wall behind

The other important creation by Fokine in 1907 was *Le Pavillon d'Armide*. Designed by Alexandre Benois to evoke the court of Louis XIV, the ballet again evolved over performances. On 25 May Pavlova danced as Armida in the one-act version, and when the three-scene version was prepared for the Maryinsky for 25 November, and Kschessinskaya dropped out at the last minute, Pavlova again assumed the title role. This does not appear to have been one she particularly enjoyed, and the ballet was more significant for Nijinsky's appearance in the virtuoso role of Armida's slave. An important series of photographs shows these two charismatic stars together in this ballet; it was one of these which appeared hand-tinted on the cover of the periodical *Le Théâtre* (No. 249) in Paris in early May 1909, advertising Diaghilev's 1909 Saison Russe.

Pavlova continued to work with Fokine early into 1908, and on 8 March she created the dramatic role of Veronica, a young girl in love with the misguided hunter, Amoun, who has fallen in love with Cleopatra in the ballet *Egyptian Nights*. For Paris the following year Diaghilev would transform Veronica into Ta-hor and *Egyptian Nights* (which ended happily) into the tragedy of *Cléopâtre*. This to some extent brought Pavlova's involvement with Fokine to an end, for at the close of the season at the Imperial Theatre Pavlova was one of 23 dancers to tour to the Baltic countries and Central Europe with the impresario Edvard Fazer. Although she added Odette in *Swan Lake* (the lakeside scene) to her repertory for Fazer's tours, the productions were largely ones she had memorably danced already. Touring overseas heralded a change of focus for Pavlova, a chance to take her art to new audiences rather than broaden her repertoire further. By 1909 she had completed ten years of service to the Imperial Ballet.

Fokine recognised that Diaghilev could give him a welcome opportunity to put his ideas about choreography into practice and enable his ballets to be seen by an influential new public in Paris. Indeed, over the next four seasons, 1909–12, Fokine's ballets attracted new audiences to the ballet. However, in 1912, resenting the attention given to Nijinsky and his first major ballet, *L' Après-midi d'un faune*, Fokine turned to other outlets, including Pavlova's company. Pavlova seems to have been delighted to work with him again and two productions were commissioned for her 1912–13 season at the Kroll Opera House in Berlin. The first was *The Seven Daughters of the Mountain King* set to Alexander Spendiarov's symphonic *Three Palms*. It was described in the programme as 'an Oriental version of the Niebelungen legend – for the seven daughters of the Ghost King are closely comparable to the Walküre in the second opera of Wagner's great ring'. Pavlova danced the role of a Persian Princess. The second, premiered in January 1913, was *Les Préludes*, inspired by Lamartine's *Méditations Poétiques* with music by Franz Liszt. It was a symbolic work in which Pavlova created the role of the Spirit of Love. Boris Anisfeld's Futurist set came in for criticism, and although this ballet remained in the repertoire until 1923, it was regarded as grotesque and too abstract for many audiences.

In terms of score, design and movement these two ballets were among the most radical created for Pavlova's own company. Fokine, whom Diaghilev had encouraged to keep moving forward, was seen to have gone too far with these over-ambitious ballets for Pavlova's company. Although Pavlova herself was proud of them, and brought them back to the stage (particularly when Fokine was available to rehearse them), her colleagues, as well as her audiences – many of whom were just discovering ballet – considered them too challenging and neither were frequently danced.

Although from 1910 Pavlova danced primarily outside Russia, her association with the Imperial Ballet continued until the outbreak of war in August 1914. She returned to dance at the Maryinsky early in the 1911–12 season, performing as Nikiya and Giselle, before joining Diaghilev's company at the Royal Opera House, Covent Garden. She again returned in February 1913 after working with Fokine in Berlin, repeating her roles as Kitri, Aspicia and Nikiya. Her final visit to Russia was in the summer of 1914, again after a season in Germany. As it was the vacation period for the Imperial Theatres she took a small group of dancers with her – Bergé, Oukrainsky, Plaskowieczka and two English girls, Butsova (Hilda Boot) and Crombova (Madge Abercrombie) – and presented a divertissement in popular theatres in St Petersburg (at the Narodny Dom, or Peoples' Palace, newly rebuilt after the 1912 fire) and Moscow.

The First World War and Revolution cut Pavlova off from her homeland, but she was constantly concerned for those suffering in Russia. She undertook charity performances to send aid for Russian victims of famine, and in 1920 she opened an orphanage for Russian children at St Cloud, Paris. Although she held special fund-raising performances, she personally paid for much of the cost of running the orphanage. Pavlova never lost her sense of being Russian and she valued the traditions that the Imperial Ballet had given her, traditions and skills that she would share with the next generation of dancers worldwide.

1   Nicolas Legat, *Dancing Times*, February 1931, p. 683.
2   Valerian Svetlov, 'Tsaritsa Mab', *Ogni*, No. 3 (1906); quoted in John and Roberta Lazzarini, *Pavlova: Repertoire of a Legend* (London: Collier Macmillan, 1980), p. 62.

Pavlova's entrance as the mummified Bint-Anta in *Pharoah's Daughter,* Moscow, 1906

The death of Nikiya in the betrothal scene of the
ballet *La Bayadère*, St Petersburg 1903

Pavlova in typical chiton-style
shift worn for rehearsals
in the early twentieth–century;
these allowed more
freedom of movement than
traditional tutus

Anna Pavlova

COMPANY OF HER OWN

In the first decade of the twentieth century Anna Pavlova was one of the first ballerinas from the Imperial Russian Ballet to dance in Western Europe. Although groups had performed in Monte Carlo at the invitation of Raoul Gunsbourg from 1895, it was with the tours organised by the Finnish-based musician and impresario Edvard Fazer in 1908 and 1909 that Russian dancers started to make a significant impact in the West. And Pavlova was foremost among them.

Fazer's tours took place in May and early June, immediately after the seasons at the Maryinsky had closed for the summer break. In 1908 Pavlova was un-doubtedly the star of a group that included Adolph Bolm, Evgenia Edouardova, Mikhail Obukhov, Elena Polyakova, Elsa Will, and Alexander Shiryaev and his wife Natalia Matveeva. They toured the Baltic countries, performing in Helsinki, Stockholm and Copenhagen, before moving to Prague and Berlin. In 1909 the focus was on central Europe: the dancers returned to Berlin before moving south to Leipzig, Prague and Vienna. Several of the dancers, including Bolm who was committed to Diaghilev, were no longer part of the group for the 1909 tour, but Nicolas Legat partnered Pavlova, and the ballerina Lubov Egorova (on leave from the Maryinsky for the 1908–9 season) also took part.

As Lise in *La Fille mal gardée*, 1909

1909 — MAI. — Numéro Spécial : LA SAISON RUSSE A PARIS — N° 249

LE THÉATRE

M. WAZLAW NIJINSKY, PREMIER DANSEUR. — Mlle ANNA PAVLOVA, PRIMA BALLERINA DU THÉATRE IMPÉRIAL MARIE (PÉTERSBOURG)
LE PAVILLON D'ARMIDE

ÉDITEURS : Manzi, Joyant & Cie, 24, Boulevard des Capucines, Paris. — PRIX NET : 2 fr.; Étranger, 2 fr. 50

Pavlova's two seasons with Fazer were vitally important for her career. They gave her a taste of real independence and revealed how the art of ballet as it had developed in the Imperial Theatres was appreciated by Western audiences. Her reception in Stockholm made a lasting impression, as she later recorded:

> I ventured into Scandinavia, and for the first time enjoyed the thrill of being welcomed by royalty. I looked on this as one more milestone passed on the hard road to fame: but even then I realized that where I must rule was in the hearts of the people. Still unused to renown, I could not quite understand why numbers of people began to gather outside my hotel window after the theatre each night and refused to depart until I spoke to them from the balcony. Once I remarked on it to my maid, a simple Russian peasant girl. She replied, Madame, one can easily appreciate their feelings. You make them forget for an hour their sad, hard lives, their sorrows, their poverty. They come to thank you. I have earned few tributes which I value higher than that.[1]

The realisation of the impact she had on people became central to Pavlova's career, making her determined to reach new audiences around the world. It also accounts for her willingness to meet her fans and be unfailingly gracious when leaving the theatre, often distributing flowers from her bouquets to young admirers (her stage-door appearances, like her renowned curtain calls, became an art in itself).

Fazer's 1908 and 1909 tours were also important in providing a template for Pavlova's own programming. Performances consisted of one longer ballet such as *Paquita* (with the full narrative as well as the 'grand pas'), *Coppélia* or *Giselle*, or two one-act ballets. Both styles of programme would end with a divertissement (a group of specially created solos, pas de deux or group dances – either miniature works or extracts from longer ballets). The one-act ballets on the first tour were *The Cavalry Halt*, *The Magic Flute* and *Swan Lake* Act II. The second tour dropped *Coppélia* and added *Harlequinade* (*Les Millions d'Arlequin*) and *La Fille mal gardée.* This pattern of one longer or two shorter ballets plus a divertissement was adopted by Pavlova herself for her own theatre tours. When she was presenting 'flying matinees' (day-time performances in a different town from that in which a season was being presented), or one- or two-night stands in non-theatrical halls, she avoided the use of sets and presented a full programme of divertissements. These might include a ballet such as *Chopiniana*, which was a series of dances conveying a 'romantic' mood with no specific story or setting. Although a mixed programme of dance now seems familiar, when Pavlova first came to England a full evening of dance was a rarity. Pavlova recruited some of the Fazer dancers to join her for the first London seasons: Edouardova took part at the opening of the 1910 season, while Shiryaev and Matveeva were with Pavlova in 1911 and 1912.

Much has been written about Pavlova's career in Britain and her 'break' from Diaghilev's Ballets Russes, but much of it bears little relation to fact. When Pavlova first danced in London in 1909 for private soireés she went to great lengths to understand the role of ballet in the city. In a letter to Fazer (quoted in translation in Serge Lifar's *The Three Graces*) Pavlova recognised that to perform at Covent Garden or Drury Lane would require far greater resources than she could command. She also remarked that the British public had no experience of watching programmes 'consisting wholly of ballets'.[2]

By accepting to dance in variety at the Palace Theatre and, during her seasons, to give special matinees dominated by dance, Pavlova was able gradually to introduce the British public to those full programmes of ballet. Beginning in 1911, she took programmes that initially comprised ballet and a short play, and then simply ballets, on tour throughout Britain. It was thus Pavlova, and not Diaghilev, who introduced to Britain a programme in which ballet dominated and eventually stood alone. It was she who placed the focus on dance while Diaghilev gave audiences a stunning theatrical experience. Furthermore, as

Cover of *Le Théâtre*, May 1909, showing Vaslav Nijinsky with Pavlova in *Le Pavillon d'Armide*

Poster for 1909 Saison Russe incorporating Valentine Serov's drawing of Pavlova in *Chopiniana*

Marie Rambert said in a BBC broadcast in 1970, 'Pavlova excited in people the desire to dance while Diaghilev inspired people in a love of ballet and a love of choreography'.[3]

Although it has become commonplace to say that Pavlova was conservative while Diaghilev catered for the avant garde, and therefore to dismiss Pavlova as reactionary, it is notable that the ballets audiences still flock to see in the early twenty-first century are precisely those 'classics' that were central to Pavlova's repertoire. At the same time many of Diaghilev's works (especially those not scored by Igor Stravinsky) have faded from live performance. There was a practical reason, too, for Pavlova's more conservative choices: on tour she often had to use local theatre musicians who would have been incapable of playing challenging scores.

So did Pavlova 'break away' from Diaghilev and his Ballets Russes, as is so often asserted? The question assumes that Diaghilev's company began in 1909, while in fact in 1909 and 1910 Diaghilev, like Fazer, was presenting dancers from the Imperial Ballet of St Petersburg, Moscow and Warsaw during their summer break. Diaghilev's activities were part of a wider programme of presenting Russian culture (fine art, music, opera and ballet) to audiences in Paris and Western Europe fascinated by Russia. In 1910 Diaghilev, again like Fazer, presented ballet in Berlin before returning to Paris and Brussels. By this time international theatre managers and impresarios were fighting to secure the services of great dancers, and thus Diaghilev recognised the need to establish his own company if he was to control the careers of the dancers central to his enterprise – which he did in 1911. The first

performance of the Ballets Russes took place in Monte Carlo on 6 April that year. While Paris and Monte Carlo became central to Diaghilev's enterprise, Pavlova focused instead on Britain, Germany and America (although she did give some important performances in Paris prior to Diaghilev's famous season in 1913, including starring at the new art deco Théâtre des Champs-Elysées).

The traditional perspective on Pavlova and Diaghilev also overlooks the fact that Pavlova's performances for Diaghilev's Saison Russe at the Théâtre du Châtelet in Paris in 1909 were for her just another step en route to global stardom. She joined Diaghilev when the season was well underway, having completed her engagement in Central Europe for Fazer. That Diaghilev himself placed great emphasis on Pavlova's participation is surely indicated in his use of Serov's portrait of Pavlova in *Chopiniana* as one of two images to advertise his season (the other being Chaliapin in *Ivan The Terrible*). Pavlova appeared in three ballets in the 1909 season: in the title role in *Pavillon d'Armide*, in *Les Sylphides*, and as Ta-hor in *Cléopâtre*. She also took part in the gala at the Opéra when she performed with Mikhail Mordkin in a pas de deux (to a mixture of composers but partly inspired by *The Pharaoh's Daughter*) that apparently brought the house down.

Another frequent claim is that Pavlova pulled out of the 1910 season because she disliked Stravinsky's music and therefore did not wish to take the title role in *The Firebird*. Diaghilev's collaborators seemed to assume that Pavlova would dance a role to which she was clearly suited, but it is debatable whether Pavlova ever really considered taking it on. From the summer of 1909 she was negotiating a season with her own small group of dancers at the Palace Theatre in London, to run from April to August 1910; she would therefore not have been available for either the rehearsals or the performances. It appears that Pavlova may have been trying to play various managers and impresarios off against one another. On 15 December 1909 she had signed a contract to dance for Diaghilev between 12 June and 25 July 1910 (dates which bear no relationship to the eventual Ballets Russes season).[4] Pavlova may have been uncertain that the London season would run so long, or Diaghilev may have felt that he could somehow engineer Pavlova's availability (as he eventually did with Tamara Karsavina, who was signed by Osbert Stoll for a concurrent season at the London Coliseum). However Alfred Butt, the manager of the Palace, appears to have been less accommodating. Having agreed a vast fee to secure Pavlova for the Palace, Butt was adamant she would not dance elsewhere, and although she was permitted to dance at private soirées, Butt was reluctant to release her for the occasional gala even in 1912 (although he did agree to her appearance at the gala in aid of the survivors of the Titanic at the Royal Opera House on 14 May 1912).[5]

Pavlova did, of course, dance again for Diaghilev, and this time with the Ballets Russes – but she was very definitely appearing as a guest artist. In 1911, when Diaghilev established his company, he realised that his prima ballerina, Tamara Karsavina, was not available for the full autumn season. Desperate for first-rate ballerinas to sustain his autumn season at the Royal Opera House, Diaghilev therefore invited Kschessinskaya and Pavlova to come to his aid. Kschessinskaya welcomed the opportunity to perform for new opera-house audiences, while Pavlova, who was about to embark on her first British regional tour, cannily

recognised the value of being able to be advertised as coming directly to the regions from the Royal Opera House, Covent Garden.

There appears to have been little love lost between Pavlova and Diaghilev in the years leading up to 1914. In the St Petersburg press Diaghilev claimed that Pavlova was demeaning the art of ballet by appearing in variety. He never acknowledged that she had in fact helped to pave the way in London for his own triumphant seasons, as a book published as early as 1913 makes clear: 'Nothing can well be written about the Russian Ballet without some mention of Pavlova. For though that great dancer has not been associated with the [Ballets Russes]... it is largely to her art that London owes the revived interest in ballet which paved the way for these later spectacles.'[6] Pavlova's remarkable success in galvanising interest in ballet is beyond question. Cyril Beaumont, the London bookseller and dance historian, was just one who discovered the excitement of ballet when taken reluctantly to the Palace Theatre in April 1911:

> Until then I had no conception that dancing could rise to such heights. The dancers and the music were one, and they seemed able to express every emotion they pleased. With each new dance you were swept from gaiety to spiritual ecstasy, from sadness to a wild savage delirium that made you long to leap on the stage to join in the dancing. There were times when I could hardly keep still, so passionately stirred was I by the surge and rhythm of their movements. For hours afterwards the images of Pavlova and Mordkin dominated my thoughts.[7]

Pavlova and Diaghilev clearly kept a jealous eye on one another's activities, particularly when they were appearing in major cities at the same time. There are intriguing hints that Diaghilev may have been trying to persuade Pavlova to guest with his company. In a telegram to Diaghilev in July 1921, for example, Walter Nouvel claimed that Bakst was under the impression that Pavlova would consent to dance for an unidentified season in Paris but was making conditions about including an adagio in *Schéhérazade*.[8] Nothing came of this potential collaboration but the fact that it was even considered shows how both Diaghilev and Pavlova were finding life tougher after the war. Pavlova's solution lay in regular visits to the USA and the discovery of new audiences in Australasia.

Perhaps the last word on the divisive issue of Pavlova and Diaghilev (and there are many accounts of Pavlova and Diaghilev themselves asking supporters which of the two factions they favoured) should go to Arnold Haskell, who in 1956 summed it up like this: 'Diaghilev appealed to the elite, Pavlova to the masses – and to the elite, in spite of themselves.'[9]

1   'Pavlova', *Dance Magazine*, May 1928.

2   Serge Lifar, *The Three Graces: Anna Pavlova, Tamara Karsavina, Olga Spessivtseva. The Legends and the Truth* (London: Cassell, 1959), pp. 80–82.

3   *Omnibus: Anna Pavlova (1881–1931)*, produced by Margaret Dale and first transmitted by the BBC on 25 January 1970.

4   Addenda to *Anna Pavlova 1881–1931*, catalogue of the Commemorative Exhibition organised by the London Museum in association with the Anna Pavlova Commemoration Committee, 1956, p. 4.

5   V&A Theatre & Performance Department, Alhambra 'Moul' Collection, THM/75/2/2.

6   A. E. Johnson, *The Russian Ballet* (London: Constable, 1913) p. 237.

7   Cyril W. Beaumont, *The Diaghilev Ballet in London* (London: Putnam, 1940), p. 6.

8   V&A Theatre and Performance Department, Ekstrom Collection, THM/7/2/1/1/55. Fokine had added an adagio for Zobeide and the Golden Slave when he performed *Schéhérazade* with his wife Vera for the Ballets Russes in 1914.

9   Arnold Haskell, 'Introduction', *Anna Pavlova 1881–1931*, op. cit., p. 5.

IVY HOUSE

At the door of Ivy House, 1927

Anna *Pavlova lived here 1912–1931*. The blue plaque proudly displayed since 1958 on a house in North End Road, Golders Green, marks the place Anna Pavlova chose as her home, on the northern edge of Hampstead Heath and Golders Hill Park. She chose Ivy House, according to John Betjeman, because it had 'an immense galleried hall, which she used as a practice room. There were yards of stone cellars where she stored scenery and properties. But chiefly she liked it for its garden, two acres of tree-bordered grass terracing down a steep slope to a small lake where she kept swans.'[1]

Pavlova's companion, Victor Dandré, described Ivy House as 'a typical old English mansion'. There had been a building on the site since the 1780s, but by the time Pavlova bought the house it resembled an early nineteenth-century villa with battlements, its Arts and Crafts façade probably dating from the 1880s. Previous owners included the architect and archaeologist Charles Robert Cockerell who in the early nineteenth century had unearthed a frieze at the Temple of Apollo Epicurius at Bassae which he presented to the British Museum; the casts he made from the frieze embellished several buildings including his own library, a room that became Pavlova's dining room. It was while the house was owned by Cockerell that the Romantic artist Joseph Turner had visited and 'so admired the view from the library window, that it became known as "Turner's View"'.[2] Shortly before Pavlova's acquisition, Ivy House had been owned by James Walter Smith, who added the large conservatory seen in *The Immortal Swan*, the 1929 film footage of the dancer at home. Inside the conservatory, which was later destroyed by a bomb blast in the Second World War, Pavlova constructed an aviary to house the exotic birds she brought home from her travels.

When Pavlova first came to dance in London she stayed in a hotel overlooking Hyde Park but she missed not having her own garden. After signing a regular contract with the Palace Theatre in 1911, which meant that she would be in London for considerable periods, Pavlova rented a house at Golders Green and, liking the area, looked for a more permanent base. Dandré noted, 'We did not have to look for long, for nearly opposite to where we were living, was a house with a large neglected garden to be let or sold. The stone wall round the house and part of one of the walls of the house itself were overgrown with ancient ivy.'[3] Although Golders Green became increasingly built up during Pavlova's residency, Ivy House itself retained its rural setting, with a garden that broadened out as it sloped down to a small lake.

Previous Page:
Pavlova in the bay window of
her dining room, 1927

Left:
Going up to the
terrace soon after her
acquisition of Ivy House

Pavlova loved Ivy House for three particular reasons: its garden, its facilities and its ease of access. She constantly re-fashioned the garden with trees, shrubs and flowers; adjoining the large open spaces of the park and Heath, it felt like part of the countryside. Not only was there the lake for her swans but the gardens also boasted a small lily pond with a fountain which became a favourite spot for relaxation. As Dandré recalled, 'The chief attraction of the house was its situation on the highest part of London. Each time on our return home from town in the heat of the summer we felt the freshness and difference of the air. Owing to its high situation the view from the balconies extended many miles.'[4]

Pavlova seems to have mainly spent the summers there. It was for her 'the ideal place... [a] home of peace and contentment', and many photographs survive of Pavlova either posing or relaxing in the grounds. She was a generous hostess who clearly enjoyed entertaining guests. In the summer of 1912, when she moved into Ivy House, Pavlova threw a lavish garden party that received considerable coverage in the illustrated press. (Perhaps it was no coincidence that the party was held on 13 June, just one day after Diaghilev's third London season of the Ballets Russes opened at Covent Garden.) Although she celebrated moving into the house in 1912, it was not until two years later, in 1914 (indeed, after she had left on her five-year tour of North and South America) that she was actually able to complete its purchase for the sum of £10,000.

Natalia Trouhanova, for many years ballerina at the Opéra Comique in Paris where she worked closely with Ivan Clustine, was invited by Pavlova to stay at Ivy House ten years later, in the summer of 1922, having agreed exceptionally to dance as second ballerina in Pavlova's season at the Queen's Hall that year. She found it a 'charming house ... furnished with the very best models of English taste and comfort. Anna Pavlova, who scarcely spent a month each year in her home, turned out to be an excellent and attentive housekeeper.'[5]

Ivy House also provided the facilities Pavlova needed, with a large hall to serve as a studio and basement cellars for storing sets, costumes and properties, as Trouhanova again described:

> Downstairs, in a semi-basement, were the service areas and half of this lower floor was given over to theatrical costumes. Here, in closets built in rows like cases in a library and staggered like the squares of a chessboard across the room, were stored costumes, tights, wigs, accessories, shoes and musical scores. Needless to say, there was also a card index to this material. All of it supervised by specialists: a dressmaker, laundress, hairdresser and a music librarian.[6]

The house was ideally situated for access to central London. Along streets less congested than now it was only a short drive from the theatres where Pavlova danced. The Underground station at Golders Green had opened in 1907, about ten minutes walk from the house, which, although perhaps not greatly used by Pavlova and Dandré, was ideal for the young students and company members who came for classes or rehearsals. Hilda Munnings, later more famous as Lydia Sokolova, one of Diaghilev's leading character dancers, recalled taking lessons from Pavlova and her ballet master Shiryaev in 1912: 'Golders Green was lovely in those days. From the Station you walked up the hill, which had huge trees on both sides. There was no traffic: it was a country lane.'[7] As she recounted almost half a century later, Sokolova had just returned from the USA where she had danced on Mordkin's All Star Imperial Russsian Ballet tour:

> When I entered Ivy House ... everything seemed so cool, white, shady. The French windows were wide open with sun-blinds pulled down over them. There were big vases of flowers, and perfume everywhere. The studio was awe-inspiring and seemed to me almost sacred. It was in the centre of the house: not quite square, two storeys high, and with a gallery running round it. Off this gallery with its pretty railing, white doors led to Madame's

Previous Page:
With her swans (Jack and Clara) and flamingos on the lake at her last photocall at Ivy House in 1930

Left:
Posing by an urn in the garden at Ivy House prior to her last regional tour of Britain

Right:
Tea with Enrico Cecchetti
in the garden, 1927

Below:
With Dandré at the lower end
of the garden

Above:
Pavlova in 1912; she was often
photographed with her pets

Left:
Playing croquet with Laurent
Novikoff and Fyodor Chaliapin, 1923

Above and right:
With pupils at Ivy House, 1913

Above:
Pavlova, Grace Curnock, Helen
May, Beatrice Griffiths, Muriel
Popper (Stuart), Masie McDonald.
Steinberg's painting has been
brought to Ivy House, 1913

Right:
(standing) Mabel Warren,
Curnock, Aileen Bowerman,
Beatrice Beauchamp,
Stuart;
front: (seated) Griffiths, Pavlova,
June Tripp

bedroom, boudoir and bathroom. Below was a barre. On the opposite side to the front door, windows opened onto the garden, and round the room there hung several life-size paintings of Pavlova in her famous roles. Although the sun poured in at the upper windows, down below there was a sense of coolness which I shall always associate with Pavlova.[8]

The fact that Ivy House had a small ballroom, ideal for a ballet studio, encouraged Pavlova to establish her school there. In 1913 Philip Richardson, the editor of the *Dancing Times*, visited her at ten o'clock one morning to watch her 'take a class of more or less beginners for two hours'. He described the room as a studio with 'walls lined on three sides with numerous engravings and pictures, including several original designs by Léon Bakst for the ballet, and there was a page from a "Confessional Book" signed by Marie Taglioni in December 1872. There were several engravings of Taglioni, whom Pavlova considered one of the greatest dancers ever seen.'[9] Pavlova selected eight young girls to train, none of whom had a serious dance background. It seems that she was assisted in putting the group together by Hilda Bewicke; the selection of the girls was made, after examining their feet, by asking them to move to music. As one of the successful pupils, Muriel Stuart (originally Muriel Popper), recalled: 'Slowly, through the months of auditions, once a week, she found the eight of us, but they were not her ideal eight. Her first idea was to find girls of various nationalities: English, French, German, Polish, etcetera.' While in London Pavlova took an active role in training the little group but when on tour she asked others, including the young ballerina Phyllis Bedells (who lived nearby), to deputise. Pavlova's ballet staff, including Alexander Shiryaev, taught classes and at times there were more than the select eight present. For those girls the privilege of working with the ballerina never left them, though, as Muriel Stuart appreciated, they had much to live up to:

Ivy House at the time of
Pavlova's death in 1931

Opposite left: the house viewed
from the lake; *opposite below* the
hall used as Pavlova's studio;
above the dining room;
below the entrance hall leading
to the inner hall, decorated with
evidence of Pavlova's travels
and a print of Paul and Marie
Taglioni in *La Sylphide*

Usually, she was kind, but we could tell in advance if she was in a good mood. If she wore her white Grecian robe, it was more or less a good day. But when she came in that black crepe thing ... oh! We tried her patience ... As I look back, I wish we had had someone to prepare us for her ... she was such a supreme example of grace and poetry.[10]

Her ballet staff assisted with the teaching and at the end of the 1912 and 1913 seasons the group was given the opportunity to dance with Pavlova in special performances at the Palace Theatre.

Having chosen Ivy House as her home, Pavlova shipped over her furniture from Russia and the house gradually filled with evidence of her travels. She loved to re-landscape the garden, and her gardener was kept particularly busy in the brief periods Pavlova was at home. In 1928 she had the decaying wooden terrace and balconies of the house remodelled and the garden redesigned by Percy Cane. It is this version of Ivy House which features in her home movies and is well documented in the photographs included in the elaborate prospectus produced by Folkard & Hayward for the house's sale by auction on 4 June 1931.

The history of Ivy House since Pavlova's death is a sad one. Russian authorities contested Dandré's right to inherit the property and he could produce no evidence of being legally next of kin. The Russians won their counter-claim, officially on behalf of Pavlova's mother who was still alive. Dandré had removed some material – a significant collection of Pavlova's costumes and artefacts were donated to the Museum of London but the bulk of her possessions were put up for auction. The auction catalogue, like the prospectus for the house, provides a fascinating insight into Pavlova's life.

The House was finally sold in September 1932 to the Manor House Hospital (Industrial Orthopaedic Society). During the Second World War it became the outpatients department, but in 1957 it was converted into a rehabilitation centre. It was at this time that the interior of the building, which Pavlova had so loved, was destroyed. Only two years after it was converted for 26 patients the building was regarded as redundant. In September 1962 it reopened as the New College of Speech and Drama with a small theatre built in the grounds. The College was eventually absorbed into Middlesex Polytechnic, now University. No longer needed, Ivy House was sold again in 1992.

In 1974, when Ivy House was owned by Middlesex Polytechnic, it opened on Saturday afternoons as the Anna Pavlova Memorial Museum, displaying furniture loaned by Alicia Markova, as well as photographs, prints, music, one of Pavlova's travelling trunks, elements of costumes and other memorabilia. It became a place of pilgrimage for visiting dancers, for Pavlova's fans from all over the world, and for those who continued to discover and become fascinated by the great ballerina. The museum survived for sixteen years thanks to the commitment of its curators, John and Roberta Lazzarini, and their successors from 1987 to 1990, Leonard Newman and Geoffrey Whitlock. Although there were dreams that Ivy House would survive as a Pavlova Museum or an International Dance History Centre, funds were never forthcoming. Instead it was bought to become the London Jewish Cultural Centre, the capital's leading provider of Jewish education and culture. Aware of the building's special heritage, the Centre presents a lively Music and Dance Programme, inviting stars from the worlds of classical music and dance to teach and perform in the home Pavlova loved.

1 John Betjeman, 'Ballet-Goer's London Guide 4', *Ballet*, Vol. 12, No.1, March 1952, p. 33.

2 Leonard Newman, *Ivy House A Brief History of the House made World Famous as the Home of the Legendary Ballet Dancer Anna Pavlova* (London: privately published, 1992)

3 Victor Dandré, *Anna Pavlova, In Art and Life* (London: Cassell, [1932]), p. 44.

4 Ibid.

5 Natalia Trukhanova [sic], 'Anna Pavlova, a remembrance', trans. All Klimov and Alison Hilton, *Dance Magazine*, January 1976, pp. 44–50.

6 Ibid.

7 Lydia Sokolova, *Dancing for Diaghilev: the Memoirs of Lydia Sokolova*, ed. Richard Buckle (London, 1960), p. 2.

8 Ibid.

9 P.J.S Richardson, 'Pavlova: Some Memories', *Dancing Times*, February 1931, p. 690.

10 Marian Horosko, 'Pavlova and Muriel Stuart', *Dance Magazine*, January 1976, pp. 63–64.

With tulips after Pavlova
returned to Ivy House,
Spring 1920

PAVLOVA
CONQUERS BRITAIN

*"I have always dreamed of spending
the second half of my career abroad..."*

Posing in costume for
La Nuit; the flowers used
in early performances of
this solo were either lilies
or marguerites

DOVER ST. STUDIOS   **ANNA PAVLOVA.**   63.N.
THE CELEBRATED RUSSIAN DANCER.   BEAGLES POSTCARDS.

LA NUIT

I n a letter written in August 1910, well after she had first tasted success outside Russia, Pavlova wrote, 'I have always dreamed of spending the second half of my career abroad... I worked honestly in St Petersburg for ten years, and I shall leave behind a memory of myself as a good artiste and give the young dancers an opportunity to perform all the best roles. At the same time I will show Russian art abroad ... while I am still a young dancer.'[1] Pavlova was 29 and probably at the peak of her career when she wrote this. She had fulfilled her contractual engagement: dancers trained at the Imperial Ballet were expected to remain with the company for a decade. She had shone in the leading roles in the repertoire created by Marius Petipa and had enjoyed working with the master choreographer at the end of his long career. She had also worked closely with Mikhail Fokine, although his attention was increasingly focused abroad. It was time to look for new horizons, particularly while lucrative contracts were on offer for American tours and seasons in London.

Over the previous decade the fashion for what was seen as 'traditional' Russian culture had grown in Western Europe; to this was added a fascination with new Russian music and the bejewelled colours and exoticism of designs by Léon Bakst. For Pavlova the time was ripe to conquer new worlds, particularly as in 1909 she had found her ideal partner: the strong, virile Mordkin, the perfect foil to the ethereal, feminine Pavlova.

After Diaghilev's Paris season, Pavlova and Mordkin were engaged to appear at private functions in London. On 12 July they made their British debut at the home of Mrs Potter Palmer at Carlton House Terrace and a week later, on 19 July, they danced at a private party given by Lady Londesborough, where Pavlova performed three dances in the presence of King Edward VII and Queen Alexandra. In her Bakst-designed romantic tutu Pavlova danced with Mordkin to music by Chopin, followed by Rubinstein's free-flowing *La Nuit* for which

In costume for the *Russian Dance*
in her studio at Ivy House

11719 B ROTARY PHOTO. E.C.   ANNA PAVLOVA   FOULSHAM & BANFIELD

Above and opposite:
Pavlova's costume for
the *Russian Dance*

Relaxing with Mordkin in costumes
for the *Russian Dance*, 1910

Pavlova held white lilies and wore a flowing 'greyish-blue' chiton-style tunic. The third dance at this party was a *Russian Dance* Mordkin had arranged for the two of them for a charity gala in Paris in June. The dancers were then presented to the King, and the Queen asked Pavlova whether she knew the popular dance, the 'Paraguay'. Still wearing her heavy, jewelled gown and elaborate *kokoshnik*, Pavlova performed it for them. This social dance was also performed during the first Palace season.

While in London Pavlova started to look into the dance scene and discussed potential engagements with theatre managers. She discovered that although London had many theatres, and particularly music halls, the art of dance was in great need of revitalisation. In the last quarter of the nineteenth century dance had been abandoned at the opera house as an independent art and only survived in opera-ballets. Meanwhile it had flourished within a music-hall and variety setting. This was ballet catering to a new audience, one that as a result of industrialisation and urbanisation was growing, and increasingly mobile thanks to the development of the railways. From the 1860s dance had flourished in music halls; from 1884 the Alhambra in Leicester Square had made ballet central to its programmes, which were quickly copied by its neighbour, the Empire. It is easy to dismiss the ballet in these theatres as somehow second rate, but for a while it commanded international respect and attracted a rostrum of great Italian dancers, including Emma Bessone, Carlotta Brianza, Pierina Legnani and Enrico Cecchetti, all of whom exerted considerable influence in St Petersburg on Pavlova's generation of dancers.

By 1900 the two Leicester Square Palaces of Variety had been joined by the Palace Theatre and the newly opened Hippodrome, followed five years later by the London Coliseum. All frequently presented dance, with academic ballet being just one strand. With the arrival of Russian dancers, ballet came back into focus. These included Adolph Bolm and Lydia Kyasht at the Empire in 1908; Tamara Karsavina, Maria Baldina and the Kosloff brothers at the Coliseum in 1909; Lydia's brother Georgii Kiaksht (*sic*) and Ludmilla Schollar at the Hippodrome later in 1909, with Olga Preobrajenska and Ida Rubinstein following; and, finally, Ekaterina Geltzer and Vasily Tichomiroff at the Alhambra for Gorsky's ballet, *The Dance Dream*, in 1911. Apart from the partnership of Bolm and Kyasht, and the initial visit by Kiaksht and Schollar, most of these stars came to London with small supporting groups during the summer break from the Imperial theatres. The majority of the Russian dancers remained in London and only the Kosloffs' company, after performing in the USA, seriously toured Britain, as Pavlova did, their success owing more to their pirated version of *Schéhérazade,* a ballet of sex and violence set in a harem, than to individual dancers.

The Palace Theatre of Varieties, Cambridge Circus, where Pavlova was engaged, had been built in 1891 for Richard D'Oyly Carte as the Royal English Opera House. In May 1892 Sarah Bernhardt had presented a season there, but in October its new owner Augustus Harris secured a license to turn it into a variety theatre. When it opened as such on 10 December 1892 its programme included ballets with choruses, since Harris felt that audiences needed help to follow the narrative. The inclusion of ballets was short-lived but there was often at least one dance act on the bill. These included Aenea (the aerial dancer) and

Luigi Albertieri (Cecchetti's 'foster son' and protégé) in *The Spider and the Fly*; Nini Patte-En-l'Air's quadrille for which Toulouse-Lautrec designed a poster; and Léon Espinosa's ballet *La Pastorale* for Emma Palladino. Loïe Fuller, Minnie Thurgate, De Dio and a number of Spanish dancers, including Rosario Guerrero and La Tortajada, also performed there. In 1908 Maud Allan became the sensation of the Palace with her rippling arms and Salome dance, complete with the severed head of John the Baptist. Allan achieved her two hundred and fiftieth performance at the Palace on 14 October, but nine days later sprained her ankle, which brought the season to a close (although she returned the following year). Allan's success was significant for it was for her that Alfred Butt, who had become the manager of the Palace in 1904, introduced the Wednesday matinees to showcase her dancing. These he would also make a feature of Pavlova's seasons. Matinees enabled a wider selection of a dancer's repertory to be presented than was possible in the usual half-hour slot in the evening programme.

During the years in which Pavlova became the star dance attraction at the Palace, 1910–14, other dance acts included Maud Allan, Lady Constance Stewart Richardson, Stasia Napierkowska (later a silent-screen movie star), Tortola Valencia and various troupes of Tiller Girls. Also featured was the Anglo-Indian Roshanara (Olive Craddock) who pioneered Indian dance on the British stage and who toured with Pavlova dancing her own 'Indian' Dances in 1912–13. Diaghilev presented Roshanara in *Schéhérazade* in London, and she eventually worked with Adolph Bolm's multi-national company in the USA. Vaslav Nijinsky was booked to replace Pavlova in 1914 but his season was cut short by ill-health. Nicolas Legat with Nicolayava danced at the Palace in 1915.

It is clear that Pavlova made a greater impact on the London scene than her contemporaries over four long seasons, but it would be wrong to suggest that an audience capable of recognising her importance and talent did not already exist. The dance community may not have been anything like as sophisticated as that in Russia, but it was possible to have a basic training. When her Russian colleagues returned home or found alternative employment, Pavlova managed to build up her company with English girls. Hilda Boot (Butsova), who joined Pavlova in 1912, had trained at the Steadman Academy in London. Others, including Rita Leggierova, who joined a year later from the Alhambra ballet, had trained with Lucia Cormani, Elise Clerc and Alexander Genée, teachers closely associated with the Alhambra and Empire. In addition, some of the dancers who came to London initially to appear with other groups in other theatres, including Laurent Novikoff, Alexander Volinine and Catherine Devillier, were absorbed into Pavlova's company.

On 18 April 1910, having just returned to Europe from their first American appearances, Pavlova and Mordkin performed at the Palace for the first time. Audiences were stunned by their dance partnership. The programme was completed by ten other dancers, led by Edouardova and Monahoff, who presented a repertoire of Russian dances, mazurkas and Liszt's *Rhapsodie Hongroise*. The season ran for three and a half months until 6 August and included Wednesday matinees in which ballet predominated.

Initially Mordkin made as strong an impact as Pavlova. Appearing in the USA and Britain before Nijinsky, he was acclaimed as the greatest male dancer of his time, but it was his appearance even

10501—19   PALACE. LONDON.   ROTARY PHOTO, E.C.

The façade of the Palace Theatre
advertising appearances by Pavlova
and Mordkin in 1911

M. MORDKIN.

ANNA PAVLOVA.

THE PALACE THEATRE.

Week Commencing MONDAY, JUNE 5th, 1911, at 8 p.m.

GRAND WHIT-MONDAY MATINEE.

SAISON RUSSE.

ANNA PAVLOVA

AND

M. MORDKIN,

Russia's acknowledged greatest Dancers and the famous Leaders of the Imperial Russian Ballet, supported by a specially selected Company of

Premières Danseuses

From the Imperial Opera House of ST. PETERSBURG and MOSCOW.

First Appearance in England.
MARIE FENTON,
America's Favourite Coon Singer.

THE HARMONY FOUR.

KITTY DALE,
Vocalist.

OWEN CLARK,
Original Magician.

A NEW SERIES OF FANTASTIC DANCES,	**LA PIA.**	THE SPIRIT OF THE WAVES.

REYNOLDS & DONEGAN,
Whirlwind Skaters.

OLLIE YOUNG
AND
MISS APRIL,
Soap Bubble Jugglers.

LAURI WYLIE,
Mimicking Mannikins.

THE DERBY, Etc., ON THE BIOSCOPE.

MARGARET COOPER
And Her Piano.

ALBERT WHELAN,
The Australian Entertainer.

9th & 10th SPECIAL MATINEES,
Wednesday and Thursday Next, at 3 o'clock.
ANNA PAVLOVA and M. MORDKIN, supported by a specially selected Company of Premières Danseuses.
On this occasion several additional dances not possible in the evening programme will be presented.
Margaret Cooper and Albert Whelan will also appear at this Matinee.
THERE WILL BE NO SMOKING.

THE PALACE ORCHESTRA - CONDUCTOR Mr. HERMAN FINCK.
Matinee every Saturday at 2 p.m. Full Programme. Reduced Prices.

Above and opposite:
Fliers for the 1911/12 season
at the Palace

more than his dancing that attracted comment. He was repeatedly described as resembling a Greek sculpture.

> He is an extremely handsome, well-built man, with powerful limbs, which he uses with great suppleness. He dances in his bare legs, so that you can see the movement of each muscle.[2]

The Pavlova-Mordkin duets were the highlight of the season, particularly the Dionysian *Bacchanale* (sometimes called *Autumn Bacchanale*) and *Valse Caprice* which alternated as the climax of their performances, revealing the strong chemistry between the two. Both were modern works in which Pavlova wore tunics rather than tutus, both were performed with a sense of joy and abandon, and both satisfied an audience passionate about 'Greek dance' à la Isadora Duncan as well as lovers of formal ballet. The works were adapted from choreography by Mikhail Fokine and Nicolas Legat, two of the most forward-looking Russian choreographers (although at this stage the *Bacchanale* was credited on programmes to Mordkin). Danced to music from Glazounov's *The Seasons*, the *Bacchanale* was praised for 'the magic of music and rhythm ... the joy, the sheer mad beauty of grace and motion' of a dance that 'reels into the senses'. 'Here is a vision of love and forest revelry, of fauns and rhapsody, and wood nymphs wild and shrieking in some Pagan Saturnalia.'[3] The *Stage* emphasised that 'both Mlle. Pavlova and M. Mordkin act as well as dance, and while one is fascinated by the thistledown lightness and gracefulness of their movements, one can also read a whole world of emotion and fancy in their facial expression'.[4]

Their two other duets were the so-called 'Bleichmann' pas de deux and Mordkin's *Russian Dance*, for which they wore their jewel-encrusted costumes, presenting a very different exoticism. The Bleichmann was a rather mixed affair, for after the adagio to music by Julius Bleichmann, their solos were danced to Tchaikovsky and Delibes. Pavlova's tutu was a variant on a costume designed by Prince Shervachidze for Mathilde Kschessinskaya, while Mordkin bared his legs in a Roman-style mini kilt. Other works produced for the partnership included *Les Amours de Diane* in which Pavlova danced three solos as the hunter-goddess, while Mordkin as Endymion and Petroff as a Faun vied for her attention.

Needless to say, the last named stands no chance in the game of love as it is played in fascinating, lithesome movements at the Palace, and, after a series of beautiful dances, solos, duets and trios, the amorous disciple of Pan is trampled under foot by Diane and his successful rival.[5]

The first season at the Palace was hugely successful and Sir Alfred Butt was delighted to have secured Pavlova for the next three seasons. He later recalled, 'I brought her to London at £160 a week; she achieved in a single night the greatest success of any artist in my memory. She was a sensation overnight and soon I was paying her £1,200.' Mordkin had negotiated his own contract, but from her fee Pavlova was responsible for paying the other members of her company, as well as expenses for productions.

It is perhaps not surprising that Mordkin became jealous of Pavlova's success and the second season was rife with tension. At the end of the first week, for reasons never fully explained, Pavlova slapped Mordkin and for several weeks thereafter the couple refused to perform together. This immediately placed greater emphasis on Pavlova's solos – Mordkin without Pavlova made far less impact. The solos were central to Pavlova's performances from 1911, and at the Palace they included *The Swan*, *Papillon* (sometimes given in the plural, though not be confused with a duet to Chopin also called *Les Papillons*), *La Rose Mourante* and *La Nuit*. *Papillon* was a fast, fiendish dance, and brief – all of 45 seconds – in which Pavlova flashed across the stage in gold and green; it was danced to music by Drigo. *La Rose Mourante* and *La Nuit* were less obvious displays of technique and more emotional in their response to the music. *La Rose Mourante*, performed in a pale pink, petaled tunic with a cap of pink rose petals on her head, portrayed the spirit of a rose whose death at the end of the solo seemed somewhat sudden.

The group of supporting dancers changed in 1911 from 1910, and again at the end of the season as many chose to go to the USA with Mordkin on what proved to be a disastrous tour. Mordkin's departure before the end of the season at the Palace meant that Pavlova had to quickly acquire a new partner. She invited Laurent Novikoff, then appearing at the Alhambra Leicester Square in *The Dance Dream*, to join her. However, she felt she needed an additional novelty, so she also invited pupils from London's two

As Columbine from
a coloured photograph
on the cover of the 1912
tour programme

leading stage schools – Lila Field and Steadman's Academy – to supply a corps de ballet of 50 children to stage a production of *Snowflakes*. Using music from the 'Land of Snow' from *The Nutcracker*, this was the first of Pavlova's adaptations of the scene.

At the start of 1912 Butt applied for and was awarded his theatre licence from the Lord Chamberlain, enabling the presentation of narrative works, and thus the 1912 season was marked by the addition of short narrative ballets. Pavlova now presented a longer slot in the evening performances and became the focus of the new repertoire. *Amarilla* enabled Pavlova to reveal her dramatic depth in a production that was less draining than *Giselle* (a ballet never considered suitable for music hall performances). To emphasise the ballerina's versatility, this was followed by the charming comic work *La Fille mal gardée*, which was also well received on tour, as a critic in Liverpool in September 1912 noted: 'It is a charming rural romance acted without a syllable being uttered, but expressed so delightfully by dance, gesture and movement that the audience followed it as easily as though everything suggested had been said.'

Late in 1911 (after appearing with Diaghilev's company at Covent Garden), and again in 1912, Pavlova undertook theatre tours to prestigious regional theatres. The programmes were similar to those of the Palace matinees, with one-act ballets and divertissements interspersed with musical interludes. Their success is indicated by the fact that the group made a return visit to five of the theatres they performed at, and even paid three visits to the Shakespeare Theatre in Liverpool. Reviews for the tour are very favourable although there was considerable criticism of the one-act plays included – audiences, it is clear, would have preferred a full evening of dance.

The 1913 season at the Palace, which ran from 21 April to 9 August, opened with Fokine's *Les Préludes*, a less happy inclusion in a variety programme. It was followed on 10 June by Piotr Zajlich's *Invitation à la Danse*, to Carl Maria Weber's famous score, which proved a useful company work. A shy but attractive debutante, attending her first ball in about 1830, is attracted to a man with whom she dances. 'As the dance proceeds their interest in each other grows, until real sentiment is formed: but as the music of the valse dies away they are forced to part, and their dawning love is ended.'[6]

During the pre-war years in London Pavlova recognised the potential of British girls to dance. In 1911, after *Snowflakes*, she began to teach her select group at Ivy House, and at the end of the 1912 and 1913 seasons she presented her pupils as part of the final matinees. She was assisted in their training by the great dance teachers Alexander Shiryaev and Enrico Cecchetti. It appears that her 'school' only really lasted those two seasons as Pavlova left for America in October 1913, although she encouraged her pupils to go to Paris and work with Ivan Clustine in her absence. Before the war there were few, if any, teachers in Britain who could produce dancers of academic ballet of an international standard schooled in the Russian style. Later, Pavlova benefited from the schools in London established by Serafina Astafieva and Cecchetti. During her wartime tours of South America she would suggest to aspiring dancers, such as Doreen Young in Chile, that they travel to London to study with Astafieva. Early autumn 1913 must have been spent rehearsing before Pavlova's company went back to the USA. Pavlova was joined by her former teacher, Cecchetti, who that season preferred to travel

Costume design by Bakst for *Oriental Fantasy*, 1913

to North America with Pavlova than to South America with Diaghilev's Ballets Russes. With his assistance, Ivanov's ballet *The Magic Flute* was mounted and previewed at the London Opera House in Kingsway, with Pavlova as Lise, Novikoff as Luke and Cecchetti as the Marquis. *The Magic Flute* was one of three ballets previewed that evening, alongside *Une Soirée de Chopin*, a new set of eleven dances to Chopin's music, and Piotr Zajlich's *Oriental Fantasy*, 'a ballet of barbaric splendour'. Designed by Bakst to take advantage of the fashion for his Arabian Nights-style designs, *Oriental Fantasy* was similar in narrative to *Cléopâtre* and *Thamar* (popular ballets in Diaghilev's company's repertoire). An enchantress (Pavlova) lures an 'Oriental Galahad' to her palace and entertains him with music, wine and dancing, but unlike the victims in the Ballets Russes productions he has a talisman to protect him and escapes seduction. At the second 'farewell matinee', on 7 October, the company presented *Giselle*, giving Londoners a rare chance to see Pavlova in the role, alongside Novikoff as Loys/Albrecht, Cecchetti as the Prince Regent and Plaskowiestzka as Myrtha. Ten divertissements were performed, with Pavlova dancing a pas de trois with Bergé and Oukrainsky, *Le Papillon* and *L'Automne Bacchanale*.

11719 A ROTARY PHOTO. E.C.   ANNA PAVLOVA.   FOULSHAM & BANFIELD

Right:
In costume for the Bleichmann pas
de deux at the Palace Theatre, 1911

Left:
With Laurent Novikoff in *Bacchanale*

Pavlova had been away from Britain for a year and was travelling back home through Germany when, on 1 August 1914, war was declared. She and her dancers got away but her sets and costumes were impounded. Zajlich was interned in Germany; Clustine travelled from Paris to join Pavlova as she prepared to return to America. Before leaving England she gave a few regional performances, including at the Winter Gardens in Bournemouth on 5 and 6 October. At a matinee in aid of the British and Russian Red Cross at the Palace Theatre a week later, she gave the first performance in England of *Le Réveil de Flore* (*The Awakening of Flora*), arranged by Clustine with sets and costumes by the British artist Albert Rutherstone.

Pavlova had been gradually recruiting English girls for her company while in Britain, a number of whom set out to tour with her at this time, albeit most of them disguised under Russian-sounding names. Pavlova was said to like English girls as they tended to be obedient and respectful. Many were very young when they set out but she always looked out for their welfare and encouraged them to better themselves by reading good literature and taking advantage of the experiences that travel provided. Many of her male dancers were Polish, and already notable character dancers. They all had to show great resilience, sometimes in very trying circumstances, in the five years of touring that lay ahead.

The years 1909 to 1914 were years of real triumph for Pavlova. As a dancer her appeal was immediate and emotional. She captivated all sectors of society, from the aristocracy to occupants of the cheapest seats, as she toured the country. She inspired and delighted, and she opened the eyes of the British to the possibilities of ballet. As the *Evening Standard and St James's Gazette* claimed:

> The appeal of Pavlova is to all; because it is the appeal of perfection to humanity. No matter how little we know of the Art of Dancing, no matter how uninstructed we may be in all that constitutes the idea of dancing, yet the movement, the grace, and the exquisite rhythm of Pavlova win a way to every human heart by sheer force of beauty and perfection.

1 Letter from Pavlova to M. Gorshkova, 8 August 1910, quoted in John and Roberta Lazzarini (eds), *Pavlova Impressions – Presented by Margot Fonteyn* (London: Weidenfeld, 1984), p. 49.
2 'The Russians at the Palace', *Graphic*, 30 April 1910.
3 Austin Harrison, 'The Greatest Dancer of the Age', reproduced in the programme for Pavlova's regional tour of 1911 from the *Daily Mail*.
4 'The Palace', *Stage*, 21 April 1910, p. 12.
5 'New Dance at Palace Theatre', *Standard*, 17 May 1910, p. 3.
6 Reproduced in the programme for Pavlova's 1912 tour.

Curtain call at the
London Opera House, 1913

Overleaf:
Pavlova's arrival at Liverpool, 1912

ANNA PAV
ARRIVAL AT L'POOL

SPECIAL TRAIN
AND
ᴸᴬVLOVA COMPANY ON TOUR

BUCHANAN'S

BUCHA
SCO

ᴸOVA.
ᴇPT. 1912.   1.   Carbonora
                        L'pool.

Amarilla was the first one-act narrative ballet created for Pavlova and her company at the Palace Theatre in London. It was first performed on 5 June 1912. Its plot, and in all probability its dances, drew on the dramatic ballets Esmeralda and Giselle, in which lower-class girls are betrayed by noblemen; it was created to show Londoners Pavlova's skill as a dramatic ballerina.

AMARILLA

Studio portrait as Amarilla, 1912

marilla is a Gypsy who is cast off by her former aristocratic lover after he seduced her while pretending to be a simple peasant. She is brought to entertain at a *fête champêtre* and to tell the fortunes of a Count and the Countess he is about to marry. The troupe of Gypsies dance in the gardens of a chateau and Amarilla fails to recognise the Count as her former lover until she is telling his fortune. Suddenly the recognition is mutual and the Count indicates to her that he can know her no longer. Amarilla performs a lively dance hoping she will win him back but he leaves with the Countess on his arm. Left alone, Amarilla hopes he will return but when he does it is only to coldly give her a purse of gold.

Amarilla was created when Pavlova returned to London with Novikoff as her partner. As talented as Novikoff undoubtedly was, Pavlova must have been aware that their partnership was not as powerful as her one with Mordkin. She needed to develop other aspects of her performance. Restrictions preventing narrative works being presented in music halls had recently been lifted, and Alfred Butt clearly felt that *Amarilla* was an important enough production to commission an elaborate set by the French artist and illustrator Georges Barbier. The impressive view of parkland, with stairs and a terrace, was also used for the official artist photographs. Within a month of *Amarilla's* creation, on 1 July 1912, Pavlova and Novikoff also performed in variety's first Royal Command Performance in the presence of George V and Queen Mary, presented at the Palace Theatre.

Amarilla was arranged in 1912 by the Polish dancer and choreographer Piotr Zajlich. Later performances are credited to Clustine, but this is indicative of the continuing nineteenth-century practice of crediting the ballet master who rehearsed a production rather than the original choreographer who created or arranged the steps. There is no evidence that the choreography changed significantly over its eighteen years of performance. The music was selected from existing scores by Alexander Glazounov, Riccardo Drigo and Alexander Dargomyzhsky, rather than being newly composed.

Georges Barbier's sets and costumes were loosely based on the style of the French rococo artist Jean-Antoine Watteau (1684–1721), noted for his wistful *fêtes galantes*. Barbier is best remembered for his stylish art deco fashion plates

Costume worn by Pavlova
as Amarilla

M. STOLVITTS

GEORGE BARBIER 1914

ALEXANDRE VOLININE

GEORGE BARBIER 1914

Mᵉˢ LINDOWSKA.

GEORGE BARBIER 1914

as well as the portfolios he produced on the Ballets Russes dancers, Tamara Karsavina and Vaslav Nijinsky. He was clearly given the chance to re-think the production after Pavlova returned from America to Europe in 1920, and these updated costume designs (which reflect the brief post-war fashion for dresses based on crinolines) were reproduced in an album of lithographs entitled *Georges Barbier: 25 Costumes*. Barbier's original 1912 sets and costumes would have appeared rather traditional when contrasted with the more avant-garde work by Léon Bakst, but they fit distinctly with designs for late music-hall ballets in London.

The initial cast was impressive, with Novikoff partnering Pavlova as Amarilla's brother, Inigo (in America the role of Inigo would be taken by Alexander Volinine). The Countess and Count were created by Anna Pruzina and Lev Laschilin, and the Gypsy chief by Shiryaev. The quartet of Gypsy women were Devilière, Gashewska, Shelepina, and Plaskowieczka, while the young Polish virtuoso, Stanislas Idzikowski, was one of the guests. The significance of the work can be appreciated by the fact that Foulsham and Banfield, who specialised in theatrical photography, were commissioned to take a series of posed on-stage photographs of the production – something that was quite unusual for the Palace at the time.

Amarilla remained part of Pavlova's repertoire right up to her last performances at Golders Green in 1930. With many one-act productions Pavlova would hand on the lead to a soloist, but she retained Amarilla for herself. The critic of the *Westminster Gazette*, who revisited the ballet when it was staged at Covent Garden in September 1924, considered it 'quite one of the finest things in the whole of Pavlova's repertoire' and appreciated that Pavlova herself was 'uncommonly fine, and in a way so totally different from that of her more usual impersonations'.[1] The following year *The Times* was similarly enthusiastic about Pavlova's performance as the betrayed Gypsy:

> It was so wonderfully done that we could for the moment believe absolutely in the conventional situation. Her drooping arms and faltering legs, that yet never make an ugly movement, conveyed perfectly the despair of the girl. Most wonderful of all was her backward run en pointes across the stage with her head thrown back. She drifted along, with just a suggestion that she might sink to the ground at any moment, yet with all the appearance of it being the easiest thing in the world to do.[2]

1 'Pavlova in a new mood. A Passionate Young Gypsy',
 Westminster Gazette, 12 September 1924.
2 'Amarilla: Madame Pavlova at Covent Garden',
 The Times, 1 October 1925.

Costume designs
by Georges Barbier for *Amarilla*, 1920
Clockwise from top left:
Une dame du chateau, the Count
(Le fiancé), the Countess (La fiancée),
Inigo (Le bohémien)

Siblings Inigo and Amarilla (Novikoff and Pavlova) dance with a tambourine watched by the engaged Countess and Count (Pruzina and Laschilin), the guests, gypsies and peasants; the Gypsy Chief (Shiryaev) is on the stairs

This page and overleaf:
Photographs by Foulsham & Banfield, London, 1912

Inigo, Amarilla's brother (Novikoff), offers a hat for the collection to the
Countess (Pruzina) and Count (Laschilin), while the four gypsy women
(Devilière, Gashewska, Shelepina, Plaskowieczka) dance with the Gypsy
Chief (Shiryaev) centre stage. Amarilla (Pavlova) on the right with
playing cards is telling fortunes for the guests. Behind are the two female
peasants in striped skirts (Matveeva and Wishniakowa)

Amarilla (Pavlova) lingers on the left by the rustic bench as the Count
(Laschilin) appears to hold back to speak to her as the guests leave

TWENTIETH CENTURY
ICON

Anna Pavlova was an instantly recognisable face in early twentieth-century media. She travelled all over the world and featured widely in the national and local press, but she was also regularly seen in illustrated theatre, fashion and society periodicals. Always well turned out and charismatic, loved by the camera as well as by her fans, for twenty years Pavlova's image was used to sell everything from cosmetics to pianos. She was one of the first icons of the twentieth century.

Studio portrait of Pavlova in a contemporary fashion outfit, 1909

Pavlova took her responsibilities as a star seriously and was always stylishly dressed, aware that she was constantly on public show. She was frequently photographed both in studios and on tour and these images reveal her individual taste and style. She appears to have chosen her outfits for comfort and practicality, and for the two decades of her international career it is possible to trace how fashions changed radically for a touring artist.

When Pavlova first toured Western Europe in 1908 and 1909, belle-époque fashions were still evident. A striking studio portrait of Pavlova (*left*) shows the dancer dressed in the epitome of contemporary fashion with a large, lavishly decorated hat, lace-trimmed bodice and trained skirt. Nevertheless, Pavlova's uncorseted dancer's body did not lend itself to the 'pouter pigeon' or S-bend silhouette of the first decade of the century, but rather to the leaner silhouette of the early 1910s, with its straight lines, slender skirts in light fabrics and smaller plumed hats. This new look comes over clearly in the photographs taken of her at her 1912 garden party to celebrate the acquisition of Ivy House, which featured widely in London's illustrated periodicals (*right*). The hostess herself wore a dress of the 'palest mauve with its sash in powder blue and bodice band in cerise', echoing the shades of the sweet peas that adorned the table.

As a charming hostess at 'one of the most delightful garden-parties ever held in London', Ivy House, 1912

By 1913 Pavlova had become a household sensation in Britain, America and Europe. With this rise in profile the public sought to know more about the life of this captivating and exotic dancer. In April 1913, to mark her return to London after her appearances at the newly opened Théâtre des Champs-Elysées in Paris, *The Tatler* featured Pavlova in a double-page spread (*above*). The central image was of the dancer in one of her most popular solos, *Papillon*, flanked by another showing her posed in a beautifully draped, floor-length gown over which she adds a fur-trimmed evening coat. The gown's high waist and curve-skimming trained skirt are both the height of fashion.

Another striking portrait of Pavlova (*right*) shows her in a floor-length, lace-trimmed dress, the epitome of late Edwardian fashion. The tight sleeves and lace bodice contrast with the long flowing skirt and the only jewellery worn is a simple pearl necklace and earrings. In this portrait it is Pavlova's stunning hat that makes the statement. This wide-brimmed confection is adorned with osprey feathers, of which Pavlova seemed to have been particularly fond. The demand for these rare feathers was such that in 1906 Queen Alexandra forbade the wearing of osprey in court (though the feathers continued nonetheless to be a much desired adornment). Hats were a particular passion of Pavlova's and even by ornate Edwardian standards she favoured the spectacular.

Anna Pawlowa

Anna Pavlova

Pavlova was always drawn to theatricality, in dress just as much as millinery. The double skirt of her dress, just visible in the photograph of the dancer (*left*), echoes Paul Poiret's 1912 design for the 'sorbet' evening gown, popularly called the 'lampshade tunic'. Poiret's wired skirts and Turkish trousers reflected the fascination for an exotic orientalism popularised by Bakst and Diaghilev in such Ballets Russes productions as *Schéhérazade* and *The Firebird* of 1910.

Leaving Ivy House for Waterloo Station to begin her journey to America in October 1913. Her velvet coat is trimmed with a deep fur collar and cuffs complemented by a fur hat adorned with feathers. Her shoes, whilst fashionable, have been chosen for comfort and practicality

In shirt, skirt, sombrero hat and fox fur with one of her dogs in New York, 1917

According to Molly Lake, who danced in Pavlova's company from 1921 to 1926, Pavlova was 'medium tall, incredibly beautifully made, with long, smooth, slim legs and narrow arched feet ... Her head was small, very dark and very smooth; her face pale, with an aquiline nose and large intensely intelligent rather than beautiful eyes.' She added that she was 'impressed by the way her plain and beautiful clothes moulded her body' and that even after overnight train journeys 'shivering on a snow-bound platform at seven in the morning, Pavlova [stepped] out of the coach aloof and elegant'.

Pavlova never aligned herself with a specific fashion house, but wore a variety of dresses. In 1914 she was photographed in Berlin (*above*) in one of Mariano Fortuny's celebrated 'Delphos' gowns, a design patented in 1909. This columnar dress of thin satin, pleated and draped from the shoulders, was inspired by the chitons of ancient Greece. The batwing sleeves were laced along the top, and the side seams of the gown were adorned with Venetian glass beads, which also helped hold the dress in place. Fortuny's elegant and non-restrictive garments appealed to dancers, including Isadora Duncan who was another of his clients at the time.

In the aftermath of the First World War fashion entered the modern era. Corsets and bustles were exchanged for dresses with shorter hemlines and increased freedom of movement. Having always favoured clothes for their practicality, Pavlova embraced these new styles. The loose, patterned dress she wore in New York (*left*) epitomises the new, freer fashions of the early 1920s. The exotic patterning on the skirt echoes that of Indian fabrics. The Orient had long been a source of inspiration and intrigue to Pavlova, who was due to embark on an extensive tour of Asia, beginning in Japan, in October 1923.

On the roofs in New York, 1923

Seasoned with a touch of fashion

Pavlova the peerless, in a lovely cloak she wore in New York. It is of green velvet trimmed with chinchilla

Pavlova's elegance was conspicuous when touring, as is seen from the above photograph in which she is waving from the window of a third-class train carriage. Posed for the benefit of the press in the autumn of 1927, the photograph shows Pavlova dressed for travel. Her simple cloche hat and tweed cloak are the perfect attire for the fashionable traveller. *Vogue* reported that 'coats designed for the happy traveller ... combine comfort, elegance and many pockets!' Pavlova spent much of her time on trains, and the UK tour of 1927 alone covered 53 towns in ten weeks and over 4000 miles. For Pavlova, who was greeted on arrival at each town, it would have been of the utmost importance to make these journeys in style.

The 1920s saw Pavlova's international fame extend as she relentlessly toured the world. She was frequently featured in the fashion pages of magazines. In the issue of the illustrated periodical *EVE* for 5 November 1925, she was photographed in New York wearing metallic shoes and an ankle-length cloak of green velvet trimmed with chinchilla, alongside the caption 'Pavlova the peerless' (*above*). Its elegance reflects Pavlova's style, now as a sophisticated woman in her early forties. The 1920s saw an increase in the demand for furs such as chinchilla, and according to *Vogue* 'rumours of threatened extinction do not prevent the continued appearance of our favourite pelts'. Indeed one of Pavlova's dancers in the 1920s, Alexis Dolinoff, recalled Pavlova having coats of mink, sable and caracul.

„Ross" Verlag

phot. Ernst Schneider, Berlin.

A photograph taken in the garden of Ivy House in the late 1920s shows Pavlova wearing a short, layered 'flapper'-style chiffon dress beneath an elegantly cut fur coat, possibly ocelot, and red-leather shoes made in Paris by A. Argence. These 'Mary Jane' shoes with their low 'Louis XIV' style heel and lattice work seem to have been a particular favourite, as she was repeatedly photographed wearing them and is likely to have had many pairs. Pavlova was notoriously fussy about her shoes. Her musical director Theodore Stier recalled that 'it was a grim day for the company when the word is passed round that Pavlova was going to buy shoes ... I knew I was doomed to long hours in a boot shop ... [as] Pavlova turned over shoes in endless variety of shape and pattern.'

Pavlova loved red shoes, often ordering several in one style; these and similar shoes feature in many 1920s off-stage photographs

For what proved to be her final photo call at Ivy House in the summer of 1930, just before she set out on her regional tour, Pavlova changed from her formal tailored outfit to wide-legged yachting pants. She teamed these with a knitted top, a look pioneered by designer Coco Chanel. Chanel's yachting pants were inspired by the bell-bottomed trousers worn by the navy and were designed to be worn at the beach or for leisure activities. The comfort and practicality of this outfit, teamed with a simple cloche hat and plimsolls, show Pavlova's eagerness to adopt new styles. She seems to have welcomed opportunities to wear trousers when relaxing in informal situations, and her willingness to be photographed like this reflects her independent spirit and openness to change.

Outfits worn in the 1920s include simple calf-length dresses with Dolman sleeves and a low belt (*above*). Her cloche hats, two-tone 'Louis' heeled shoes and simple jewellery highlight Pavlova's elegance and unique personal style. Biographer Keith Money maintains that in order to keep up with changing styles of European fashion Pavlova had many of the hems of her tailor-made pieces lifted and had several lengths of fur restyled. This in itself was not unusual and revealed her strong desire to keep up to date with the latest trends.

COMMERCE PAYS A TRIBUTE TO THE GREAT ART OF MME. PAVLOVA: A LONDON
SHOP WINDOW DEDICATED TO THE GREAT DANCER.

Mme. Pavlova, who has just completed her tremendously successful season at Covent Garden,
is now giving a series of matinées at Moss's Empires, the first being at the Leeds Empire on Monday
next, Nov. 9, and the subsequent ones at Birmingham and Cardiff; while in December she leaves for
South Africa and then will visit Australia. Our photograph shows a tribute paid by Commerce to the
art of the great dancer, as it is a shop window at Selfridge's dedicated to the incomparable Anna
Pavlova.

With her interest in clothes, Pavlova clearly enjoyed shopping, and in London
she was made welcome at the new luxury department store in Oxford Street
that Gordon Selfridge had opened in 1909. Selfridge knew how to use celebrities
to publicise and promote his emporium. One of his early gimmicks was to
display the monoplane in which Louis Blériot completed the first flight over
the Channel. Selfridge deliberately wooed Pavlova, sending her vast baskets of
flowers and ensuring her visits to 'the great house of Selfridge' were reported
in the press. The relaxed manner of shopping that he promoted obviously
appealed to Pavlova, as the *Daily Mail* described in 1911:

> So she tried on hats ... flitting from one glass to another ... moving her
> head and body to try the effect of some particular chapeau in half a dozen
> dainty poses. Selfridge's millinery department ceased to be a shop; it
> became a studio, a stage on which moved the most graceful figure in
> Europe, and the assembled attendants composed an admiring audience,
> though compelled to silent applause.

Little wonder that the delighted star declared, 'I really am certain ... that the shops
in London are the most agreeable in the world'. Selfridges returned the compliment
by devoting a window, in November 1925, to the 'incomparable Anna Pavlova' (*above*).

Other department stores also recognised Pavlova's
potential, and her name appeared in advertisements
for New York-based Barneys, and the Fifth Avenue
store Best & Co. (*above*). The extensive use of Pavlova's
name and image in the United States was most likely
the work of her American manager Sol Hurok, who
saw the vast publicity benefits that such celebrity
endorsements could create. Indeed, with the growth of
illustrated programmes and periodicals, advertisers
looked to celebrities to endorse their products and give
them cachet. The great French actress Sarah Bernhardt
(1844–1923) was one of the *fin-de-siècle* celebrities who
pioneered product endorsement, particularly when
touring the USA. Her status as an instantly recognisable
actress has a place in the pantheon of great theatrical
stars comparable to the iconic ballerina Pavlova.

MADAME
ANNA
PAVLOVA

"The Greatest Dancer of All Time," is another of the wonderful women who use and advocate Mer-colized Wax, the true complexion beautifier.

The Choice of Beautiful Women

BEAUTIFUL women and girls who value their complexion use Mercolized Wax to clear the skin, and to keep it clear. They prefer it to greasy creams, for these are liable to clog the pores and merely mask blemishes which should be removed. Mercolized Wax absorbs impurities, and thus removes all defects; it clears the skin thoroughly, leaves the pores free to breathe. Mercolized Wax is guaranteed not to contain any mercury and positively does not encourage the growth of hair; it in fact retards the growth in those with a tendency to super-fluous hair. Follow the example of these lovely clear-skinned girls who succeed in keeping a clear, fresh skin always in spite of sum-mer sun and winter wind. Begin to-night to use Mercolized Wax. Watch the rapid improvement in the health and beauty of your skin. This new beauty will have come to stay if you protect it al-ways with daily use of Mercolized Wax. Sold by your chemist in 2/6 and 5/6 packages.

Mercolised Wax for Sunburn, Freckles, Windchap, &c.

Mdlle. ANNA PAVLOVA, the world renowned dancer from the Imperial Opera House, St. Petersburg, writes concerning Odol :—

"*It gives me great pleasure to state that I have tried Odol and find it excellent for the teeth, preserving them and giving a sense of freshness to the mouth which is most agreeable, especially to one in my profession.*"

Odol possesses a distinct advantage over all other mouth-cleansing preparations, inasmuch as it not only beautifies, but also preserves the teeth, whilst the fragrant taste it leaves in the mouth is delightfully refreshing and exhilarating.

Pavlova also attracted offers from several cosmetics companies. An advertisement for Mercolised Wax appeared in the souvenir programme for His Majesty's Theatre, Melbourne, in 1929 (*above*). The beneficial effects of this product were claimed to be its mercury component (despite health warnings, the use of mercury in cosmetics continued well into the twentieth century). An endorsement for Helena Rubinstein's cosmetics featured in the programme for Pavlova's 1922 season at the Metropolitan Opera House, New York. Rubinstein, not unlike Pavlova herself, was a highly successful and established businesswoman, one of a new generation of dynamic, independent women.

Pavlova's meteoric rise on the international stage prompted a number of companies to use her name and image, not always necessarily with her permission. One of her first endorsements in England appears to have been for Odol mouthwash. Odol had been using stars to endorse their 'mouth-cleansing preparation' in programmes for many years when Pavlova proclaimed in December 1910, on the back cover of the nightly programme for the London Coliseum (a theatre at which she did not dance), that Odol was 'excellent for the teeth, preserving them and giving a sense of freshness to the mouth which is most agreeable'.

One of three advertisements for ballet shoes in the October 1921 edition of the *Dancing Times*

Advertisement for Rayne's shoes from the 1925 Covent Garden programme; and Cantilever Shoes from *The Tatler* in 1927

Whilst some of Pavlova's endorsements might have been dubious, the many adverts for ballet and day shoes were undoubtedly genuine. Like most dancers, Pavlova was notoriously particular about her ballet shoes. According to Victor Dandré, she was approached by shoemakers everywhere she went, for they were fully aware of the value of having her as a customer. Shoemakers would promise 'to provide her annually with any number for her own use free of charge, on the condition that she would allow them to advertise that she found their shoes the best'. Three advertisements for H&M Rayne, Gamba and Arthur Franks (*above*) appeared in the October 1921 edition of the *Dancing Times* and all claimed the dancer's patronage. The advert for Arthur Franks ballet shoes even ran in *Vogue*.

Pavlova's love of shoes reflected her enthusiasm for fashion. H&M Rayne used her name to promote their range of ballet and day shoes using the slogan 'Madame Pavlova wears Rayne's shoes both on and off the stage'. These advertisements appeared in the souvenir programme for Pavlova's company in the 1923, 1924 and 1925 seasons at the Royal Opera House, though Pavlova had first endorsed Rayne's as early as 1912 in programmes for the Palace Theatre, claiming their 'shoes fit perfectly'. Cantilever shoes quoted a letter from the dancer in their advertisement: 'Even our walk should be free, graceful and strong, and it can be in a shoe that is flexible like a Cantilever.'

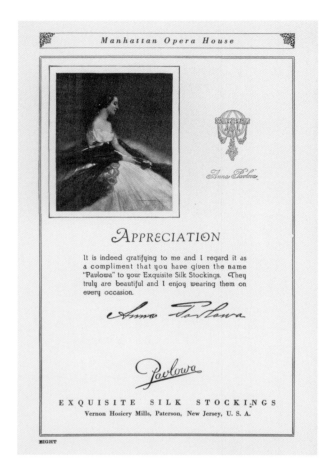

Advertisement for Exquiste Silk Stocking from the programme for performances at the Manhattan Opera House in November 1924

It was not only manufacturers of footwear that sought Pavlova's endorsement. An advert for the 'exquisite' 'Pavlowa' stocking appeared in the souvenir programme for her company's 1924 season at the Manhattan Opera House, New York. Lustre Hosiery of Australia also used Pavlova's name and image two years later to endorse its 'Silktex' stocking. However, Pavlova herself only wore silk stockings on stage and preferred cotton for everyday wear, declaring in an interview that silk was more for 'the scene' than for 'the life'.

Advertisements for Welte-Mignon and Baldwin Pianos from the programme for Pavlova's American tour; she is shown in costume for *The Fairy Doll* and *Californian Poppy* respectively

Piano manufacturers vied for Pavlova's endorsement. The Baldwin Piano Company claimed to be the 'official piano' of her company's American tours, although the company behind the Welte-Mignon reproducing piano made a similar claim. They quoted Pavlova declaring 'Wonderful, Wonderful, is the Welte-Mignon, what a musical marvel'. For the 1927 regional UK tour, it was the Bechstein piano firm that was publicised as the Pavlova company's official piano.

Right:
As company member Rita Glynde noted,
'for day wear Pavlova liked tailored suits'

Overleaf:
On tour in Australia 1929

PAVLOVA RETURNS TO BRITAIN

Anna Pavlova in *Die Puppenfee*
by Joseph Rous Paget-Fredericks

J ust before completing the acquisition of her beloved Ivy House in 1914, Pavlova deserted Britain for five and a half years. Needing to escape London and the war to find work, she did one final matinee at the Palace Theatre on 12 October 1914 in aid of the British and Russian Red Cross, and then left the country. For the next two years she worked in North America, dancing, filming, taking over the Boston Opera Company, and participating in Charles Dillingham's *The Big Show* at the New York Hippodrome. She then toured in South America, essentially travelling around the continent anticlockwise, then back the other way, adding cities such as Rio de Janiero for which a visa had not come through earlier, and finally revisiting cities on the East coast. Returning to Europe, Pavlova toured various countries, performing in Portugal and Spain for the first time, before reaching Ivy House at the end of March 1920.

The composition and repertory of her company changed during the war years. Some dancers remained in Europe for its duration and so new artists were engaged. Alexander Volinine became Pavlova's leading partner (Novikoff was now in Russia). Ivan Clustine left the Opéra Comique in Paris to become her ballet master and was responsible for most of the fairly uninspiring new productions. But from 1915 onwards it was no longer so much what she danced but where she danced that was significant. The war years were just the start of Pavlova's non-stop touring. In the 1920s she set out to conquer yet more new worlds. Tours were undertaken to Japan, China, India and Egypt, and Pavlova also visited South Africa, Australia and New Zealand. The company danced not only in the major cities but wherever they could find an approximation of a stage, and Pavlova always stressed that dancing in venues where no ballet had been seen before was as important as appearing on the more glamorous stages of international opera houses.

While touring in the 1920s, Pavlova's company varied in size according to the venues visited. Dancers were not on long-term contracts, although some remained with Pavlova for a number of years. She also employed extra dancers

Descending the stairs
backstage at the Royal Opera
House, Covent Garden, 1923

Pavlova and company at
rehearsals in 1928

Pavlova with Volinine in
Autumn Leaves, 1920

THE INCOMPARABLE PAVLOVA

Nerman captures Pavlova in her repertoire for her 1923 Covent Garden season showing
Ajanta's Frescoes, Oriental Impressions, The Swan, Japanese Butterfly and *Egyptian Nights*

for major seasons such as those at the Royal Opera House in London. For theatre tours more dancers were employed than for those presented in adapted venues such as civic halls, when divertissements were performed. For the 1922 tour to the Orient only 25 dancers and four musicians travelled with a backstage crew.

Accounts of working with Pavlova in the 1920s inevitably focus on these travels. For the young dancers the opportunity to see exotic new places and experience unusual customs and food was more memorable than what they actually danced. In 1922 and 1929 Pavlova toured in Asia, and in 1927 and 1929 Australia (in 1927 also visiting New Zealand). In 1926 she first danced in South Africa and in 1928 returned to South America. Here, reviews were more critical than they had been during the war, as people had seen a far wider range of ballet by the late 1920s. Pavlova's last visit to America was in 1924, and she returned to Germany in 1925 with long European tours in 1927 and 1930.

By the time Pavlova returned to London in 1920 there was a sense that Londoners had transferred their allegiance to the Ballets Russes. The long London seasons by Diaghilev's company at the London Coliseum, the Alhambra and the Empire in 1918 and 1919 enabled a wide audience to familiarise themselves with a more modern approach than Pavlova's. The London critics were also less enthusiastic, though even they had to admire the great ballerina.

It must have given Pavlova some satisfaction to return to London with a season at Drury Lane, a theatre she had felt in 1909 was beyond her reach. Yet while there she was eagerly signed up by the leading impresario C.B. Cochran to continue performing at his Princes Theatre (with facilities that were less than ideal for ballet). This season ran in direct competition with Diaghilev's June–July season at the Royal Opera House. Pavlova's season at Drury Lane opened with Vera Karalli, a former Bolshoi ballerina and star of many of Evgeny Bauer's films, as second ballerina. For London, Pavlova often sought out a second ballerina to carry part of her repertoire, including Sophie Fedorova (also from the Bolshoi, and with Diaghilev between 1909 and 1913), Natalia Trouhanova, and British dancers Hilda Butsova, Muriel Stuart and Ruth French.

Pavlova's programme for her return season included some of her well-loved productions, including *Snowflakes* (in a new 1915 staging), *Amarilla, Chopiniana* and *The Magic Flute. Flora's Awakening*, which had only been previewed at the 1914 gala at the Palace, was given a wider showing. To bring a more modern edge to the programme she included *La Péri* (music by Paul Dukas), and the two Fokine ballets from 1912–13, *The King's Daughter* and *Les Préludes*. And from the new works mounted in America she presented *The Sleeping Beauty* (also called *Visions*), *The Fairy Doll* (1914) and *Autumn Leaves* (1919). Pavlova also had a new personal repertory of divertissements including *Dragonfly*, *Rondo* (also called *Rondino*) and *Californian Poppy*.

In 1916, to keep her company afloat, Pavlova performed a four-tableaux version of Petipa's *Sleeping Beauty* as part of Charles Dillingham's *The Big Show* at the New York Hippodrome. The ballet was gradually cut down to become a divertissement but later two scenes became independent ballets in Pavlova's repertoire. These were *Visions* (1917) (essentially the Prince's vision of Aurora after the Hunting scene) and *Fairy Tales* (1918) (the divertissement from the last act). Pavlova's performances of these in 1920 preceded Diaghilev's famous *Sleeping Princess* at the Alhambra (November 1921–February 1922). *Visions* remained in Pavlova's repertoire and would be seen again at Covent Garden in 1924 when the *Manchester Guardian* claimed that the production 'compared quite favourably with the performances of that ballet seen at the Alhambra Theatre a few years ago. It had an artificiality less fanciful but more in keeping with the style and period of the work than the gorgeous production designed by Bakst for the Diaghilev company.'[1] From a musical perspective it was considered one of the most satisfying of Pavlova's productions.

The Fairy Doll, a ballet about toys coming to life, which *The Scotsman* described as 'a fragment fresh from Fairyland',[2] had been added to Pavlova's repertoire in America in 1914. In London it suffered by comparison to Léonide Massine's *La Boutique fantasque*, a ballet on the same theme created for the Ballets Russes in London in 1919, yet audiences greatly enjoyed it on Pavlova's nationwide tours. In 1923 it was redesigned by Sergei Soudeikine and set in a Moscow toyshop in the 1860s, with Pavlova, in her large pink spangled tutu, dancing in a memorable role.

In *Autumn Leaves* with Aubrey
Hitchens and Pierre Vladimirov

Autumn Leaves always struck a chord with viewers, no doubt because Pavlova, as choreographer, invested so much of herself in the work, insisting on extra rehearsals before almost every performance. It is a classic Pavlovan ballet in which a poet in early nineteenth-century dress rescues a chrysanthemum (Pavlova) battered by the North Wind. *The Times'* critic considered it one of the best works in Pavlova's repertoire:

> Music has been well-chosen from Chopin to fit this delicate, romantic story, and the yellows and reds of autumn make a harmonious setting. Everything fits everything else, the tempo is right, and in its short single act the different dances balance each other.[3]

It is notable that during the 1920s it was Pavlova's company rather than Diaghilev's that was seen at the Royal Opera House in Covent Garden. The Ballets Russes only performed there in the post-war years in 1920 (when they gave a season in conjunction with the opera) and 1929. Pavlova's company (independent of opera) presented four seasons – 1923, 1924, 1925 and 1927. In the 1920s ballets were presented at a number of West End theatres and were less evident in variety theatres, although the London Coliseum (at which Pavlova never performed a season) had become London's principal home of dance. Pavlova and her company had moved away from being part of someone else's programme to becoming a truly independent presentation. When no theatre was available to accommodate her company Pavlova booked it into the Queen's Hall, Langham Place (until 1941 the home of 'the Proms', the summer promenade concerts). This was not a sympathetic venue for ballet but some of the audience enjoyed a rather different perspective on Pavlova's productions. After the 1927 season at the Royal Opera House, Pavlova's company no longer danced in central London. Instead it was seen at outer London theatres in Streatham and Golders Green Hippodrome (the latter just down the road from Ivy House) as part of her regional tours.

Evidence of Pavlova's Oriental tour was present in her first season at the Royal Opera House, which opened with *Ajanta's Frescoes* (*The Great Renunciation*). This was arranged by Clustine, who had not been on the tour, although as the programme noted, 'The artistic details throughout [were] suggested by W.E. Gadston Solomon, Director of the School of Art, Bombay'. During its first season critics appear to have admired this ballet inspired by Pavlova's visit to the Ajanta caves in Hyderabad; indeed the *Daily Mail* claimed, 'This was a proper theme for a Russian ballet, and last night it was worked out with brilliance, not unrelated to corresponding scenes in *Schéhérazade* and *Le Dieu bleu*, but with a colour of its own.'[4] But therein lay its limitations, and during the same season Pavlova was to give a more precise evocation of Indian dance in *Oriental Impressions*.

The 1923 season was a feast of different cultures, for it also included *Dionysus*, *Polish Wedding* and the premiere of *Old Russian Folk Lore* (also known as *Russian Fairy Tale*). *Dionysus* was another of Clustine's efforts, a typical ancient Greek ballet redeemed by Pavlova's appearance as the High Priestess of Dionysus, the god of wine. *Polish Wedding* was a colourful folk-dance ballet inspired by descriptions of celebrations at the time of Poland's Declaration of Independence and arranged by Pianowski, though Pavlova only ever danced a few performances. (If Pavlova felt comfortable dancing works she retained them, but some she quickly handed on to another company member.)

The *Manchester Guardian* considered *Polish Wedding* to be 'a good transcription into design and colour of a real phase of national life, but the music by Krupinski was hardly adequate. It was rather unkind to play Elgar's *Polonia* overture as an introduction.'[5]

In 1912 Fokine had wanted to create his *Coq d'Or* for Pavlova's company, but with her loyalty to Russia and the tsar in pre-Revolutionary times she had put paid to the idea, and in 1914 Fokine had choreographed this opera-ballet for the Ballets Russes instead. In 1923 Pavlova turned essentially to the same folk tales for *Old Russian Folk Lore*, a ballet in one act arranged by Novikoff, in which she took the role of the Enchanted Bird-Princess. This lively ballet was regarded as one of Pavlova's more modern productions, with brightly coloured picturesque designs by Ivan Bilibine and a score described as 'modernist' by Nicholas Tcherepnine. The narrative seems to have combined elements of *Coq d'Or* with echoes of *The Firebird*, for the Bird-Princess is 'transformed into her natural shape when Prince Ivan waves a feather that has fallen from her plumage'.[6] It appears to have been a production in which other company members could shine, but there was never any escaping that Pavlova was the star. As the *Daily Telegraph* noted:

> Pavlova's first dance, as the mysterious princess, "half woman, half bird," is entrancing, but it is still more wonderful to see her lead the whole battalion of dancers at the end, doing perhaps step for step what the others are doing, and yet how infinitely lighter, more graceful, how exquisite her every movement is.[7]

If in her first seasons at Covent Garden Pavlova was slightly more adventurous, with her use of music by Alexander and Nicholas Tcherepnine, in 1924 this impression was reversed with the opening production of *Don Quixote*. Essentially reduced in the Gorsky version to a prologue and two acts, and staged by Novikoff, *Don Quixote* was new to London. It was described by the *Daily Chronicle* as 'a first act of many quick Spanish dances, all glitter and bright colours and castanets; the second act slower in general tempo, a moonlit dream scene much more suitable to Pavlova's own qualities as a dancer.'[8] With audiences now accustomed to a more contemporary view of Spain, as presented in Léonide Massine's *Le Tricorne* (1919), *Don Quixote* looked somewhat dated. Ernest Newman dismissed the music as 'utterly banal' and, apart from Korovine's sets and costumes, which he admired, found the whole rather like a ballet in a pantomime.[9] The *Daily News*, however, regarded this 'ghost of the old ballet' with nostalgia:

> Through veils of gauze one peered into the huge stage filled with beautiful girls dressed as flower-maidens – just as one imagines they were dressed in the days when Morny looked at the ballet in the Paris Opera...It was really an admirable piece of stagecraft to secure this effect. Nothing so ethereal has ever been seen upon the stage of Covent Garden. Then Pavlova, 'the queen-rose in that rosebud garden of girls,' appeared – a spirit rather than a woman.[10]

The 1925 season saw the revivals of *Giselle* and the newer ballet *The Romance of the Mummy* (inspired by the excitement around the discovery of Tutankhamen three years earlier, and drawing on *Pharaoh's Daughter*). *Giselle* was the highlight and even Newman had to admit that Pavlova's mime in the mad scene was impressive. The critic of the *Star* felt Pavlova had lost none of her qualities as a dancer:

Top left:
Pavlova as Kitri, 1925

Top right:
Giselle on stage at the Royal Opera
House, Covent Garden; an early
action performance photograph
by *The Times*

Right:
Pavlova as Kitri with Novikoff as
Basilio in *Don Quixote*, 1925

Overleaf:
The company in the revised
production of *The Fairy Doll,*
designed by Soudeikine and first
presented at the Royal Opera
House, Covent Garden on
10 September 1923

Her dancing last night, her ethereal lightness, the ease with which she does the most difficult things, were as astonishing as ever. In the mad scene she showed greater dramatic power than of old, and her dancing after Giselle has risen from the grave had the most compelling charm.[11]

As the 1920s progressed fewer new ballets were mounted and the divertissement dances were handed on from one dancer to the next as personnel changed. Even at the end of her career Pavlova was interested in the Petipa classics. Divertissements from *Raymonda* and *Paquita* were restaged, although she was unsuccessful in her plan to include the Shades scene from *La Bayadère*.

On her international tours Pavlova encouraged her company to study local dance forms, some of which were reflected in their performances. In 1919 the Mexicans seemed flattered that Pavlova and five colleagues chose to perform three traditional dances: China Poblana, Jarabe Tapatio and Diana Mexicana. The company worked with local teachers and on their first visit to Mexico City the score by Manuel Castro Padilla and sets and costumes by Adolfo Best-Martino del Rio were presented as a gift from the people of Mexico City. The colourful production contrasted well with other ballets and must have appealed to C.B. Cochran during Pavlova's season at the Princes Theatre.

Oriental Impressions (*Three Miniatures*) consisted of three Japanese dances 'arranged by Mr Koshiro Matsumo Fijima and Miss Fumi (Professors of Dancing, Tokyo)'. These appear to have left the audience somewhat bemused, although, at the gala opening in aid of the Lord Mayor's Japanese Relief Fund for earthquake victims in 1923, they admired Pavlova herself in Grieg's *Butterfly Dance*, in which she 'fluttered on to the stage arrayed as a Japanese butterfly and pirouetted about in her own inimitable fashion'.[12] This was followed by successful performances of *A Hindu Wedding* and *Krishna and Rhada*, with music by Comolata Banerji. The colour, design and the novice dancers – Uday Shankar as Krishna and Mlle Nanita – were particularly admired in *A Hindu Wedding*. As Rhada, Pavlova was fascinating and the whole production 'utterly unlike anything that Pavlova had yet given us, exotic and exquisite, solemn and sensuous, very strange in their mixture of expression.'[13]

Nonetheless, in spite of the enriching influences resulting from these travels and from Pavlova encouraging her dancers to study with local teachers, some of Pavlova's traditional repertoire – the cliché of nineteenth-century 'national' dances – began to look increasingly outdated alongside works that attempted to portray greater authenticity. Pavlova's Japanese *Butterfly* dance was one example; another was the so-called 'Chinese' dance to the 'Tea' variation from *The Nutcracker's* Kingdom of Sweets. No doubt it was because she attempted more authentic dance styles that the critic of the *Evening Standard* mused: 'I wonder how the convention first arose that stage Chinamen, and, above all, ballet Chinamen, should never show any movement without the two forefingers stretched skyward – and when will that convention die.'[14]

Although London seasons were important, it was Pavlova's British regional tours in the 1920s that were so impressive. It is difficult to build up an accurate picture, even working from programmes, press reports, diaries and letters, but Pavlova's company danced in at least 70 different places. When performing in theatres they took up to eight full ballets on tour, changing the programme half way through the week, with Pavlova usually appearing in the second of the two ballets and two or three of the divertissements.

Accounts agree that the 1927 tour was the 'toughest of all the English [*sic*] tours'.[15] Two performances were often given on a single day in different towns, with long journeys between them. Many of the stages, including the Leas Cliff Pavilion in Folkestone and the Usher Hall in Edinburgh, were dangerously slippery. The stage area in Leeds Town Hall was approached by only one entrance up a flight of stairs. The company fared better when playing full weeks in single theatres, and Algeranoff remembered the comparative luxury of the Southampton Empire with 'a fine stage and dressing-rooms, and baths and showers'.[16]

In Britain there were fewer overnight train journeys than in America or Europe, leaving the dancers with the challenge of finding accommodation. According to Algeranoff, comfortable lodgings were easier to find in Scotland than south of the border. The company's dancers were always aware that they were the supporting act for the great ballerina, but for most of them it was a life-enriching experience. They learnt from her, and they became aware of the impact she made on audiences throughout the country. Through association with Pavlova, they acquired the credentials as well as the skills to further their careers on stage or teaching. The large British contingent in Pavlova's company was thus well placed to play a key role in the development of British ballet in the twentieth century.

1   'Pavlova', *Manchester Guardian*, 12 September 1924.
2   'London Entertainments. Pavlova Ballets at Covent Garden', *The Scotsman*, 30 September 1925.
3   'Autumn Leaves. Mme. Pavlova's Ballet', *The Times*, 20 October 1925.
4   'Pavlova. Covent Garden Triumph. Entranced Audience', *Daily Mail*, 11 September 1923.
5   'Pavlova', *Manchester Guardian*, 12 September 1924.
6   'M. Tcherepnin at Covent Garden. *The Romance of a Mummy*', *The Times*, 13 October 1925.
7   'Covent Garden. A New Pavlova Ballet', *Daily Telegraph*, 18 September 1923.
8   'Pavlova Back at Covent Garden. Welcomed in ballet of *Don Quixote*', *Daily Chronicle*, 9 September 1924.
9   Ernest Newman, 'Pavlova', *The Sunday Times*, 14 September 1924.
10 'Pavlova Triumph: Storm of Welcome at Covent Garden. Brilliant Dancing and Stagecraft', *Daily News*, 9 September 1924.
11 'Pavlova's New Triumph. Wonderful Return In Covent Garden', *The Star* (Crescendo), 29 September 1925.
12 'Madame Pavlova as Priestess. Near and Far East', *The Times*, 14 September 1923.
13 'Pavlova at Covent Garden. More Ballets', *Daily Telegraph*, 12 September 1924.
14 P.P., 'Pavlova's return to London', *Evening Standard*, 24 September 1925.
15 Harcourt Algeranoff, *My Years with Pavlova* (London: Heinemann, 1957), p. 165.
16 Ibid., p. 175.

Above left and right: Mexican Dance led by
Pavlova and Pianowski

Below: Oriental Impressions with Algeranoff
and Pavlova as Krishna and Radha

Overleaf:
The Company on tour in Bremen

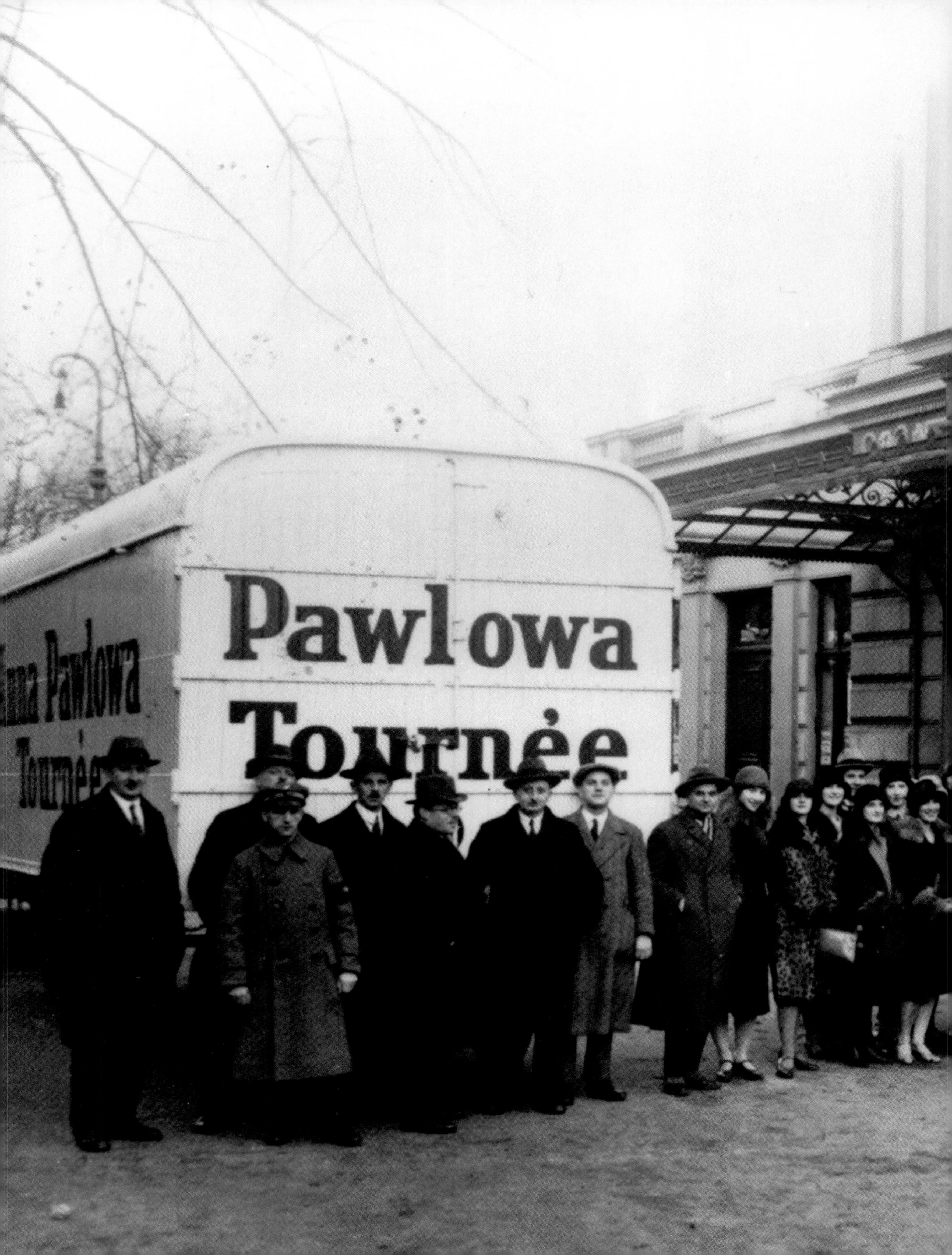
Pawlowa
Tournée
Anna Pawlowa

PAVLOVA'S "DYING SWAN" IMMORTALISED: A RARE FILM SEQUENCE.

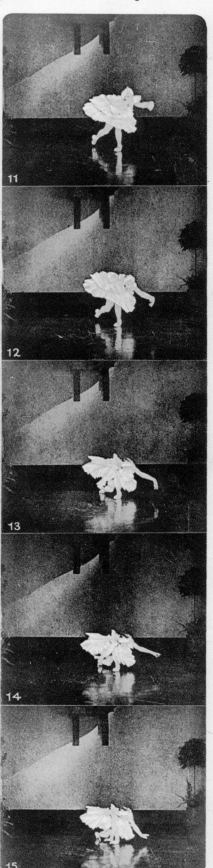

The memory of that great dancer, Anna Pavlova, is to be revived by a film portraying her life and art, entitled "The Immortal Swan." The première (postponed through King George's death) is due at the Regal Cinema on February 20. Its proceeds will go partly to King George's Jubilee Trust and partly towards the Pavlova Memorial Fountain to be erected in the Rose Garden at Regent's Park, from designs by Carl Milles, the famous Swedish sculptor, illustrated in our issue of December 14 last. The film, prepared in the British International Studios at Elstree, incorporates records which, happily, Pavlova was persuaded by Mary Pickford and Douglas Fairbanks to make at Hollywood some years before her death. They comprise four complete ballets and eleven dances, including the famous "Dying Swan," from which the above sequence is taken. The sections should be viewed in order as numbered, beginning at the top left corner.

PAVLOVA
ON SCREEN

Sequence of stills from *The Swan* as
filmed in Hollywood; published to
promote *The Immortal Swan* in 1936

"No film could possibly reproduce the fascination of the ever-changing Pavlova, or the thrill of her impact with her audience" – Kathleen Crofton 1954

In 1916 the *Manchester Guardian* declared that 'Next to seeing Pavlova in person, there is no better substitute than seeing her through the mechanism of the kinema'.[1] This, however, was not the view of those who knew the dancer and tended to be very critical of the recordings of her dancing. In 1954, at the time of a major restoration of footage of Pavlova dancing, Kathleen Crofton wrote:

> To Pavlova a performance was a living, vital experience, imbued with the freshness and spontaneity of the moment. She seemed to express an infinitude of moods and ideas; no two renderings of any role were alike. This was ever a source of wonder to those who watched her every day. No film could possibly reproduce the fascination of the ever-changing Pavlova, or the thrill of her impact with her audience.[2]

This, of course, is the dilemma faced by all recordings of dance: it is impossible to recreate the atmosphere of the live performance, and few dancers are remotely satisfied by seeing films of their own work; but for the millions who never saw a specific dancer on stage the recording does convey something of their art. There is no doubt that when footage of Pavlova is screened alongside film of her contemporaries she comes across as very different from them: she has a more modern physique and her technique is a means to an end rather than practised for its own sake.

Of course there are challenges when viewing Pavlova on film: all the footage is black and white; Pavlova occasionally disappears off camera; there is no soundtrack (sound only came in at the end of Pavlova's life and, according to Algeranoff, she experimented unsuccessfully with it in America in its early stages); and no subtle light effects could be included. Frederick Ashton, who had seen Pavlova dance in Lima and Britain, observed in an interview discussing her film performances that *Californian Poppy* in particular lost a great deal without its colour and lighting.[3] This divertissement to Tchaikovsky's *Mélodie* in E flat major, opus 42, no. 3, was inspired by seeing a field of poppies swaying in the breeze. Pavlova's solo encapsulated the day of a poppy, opening as the

Posing in her Columbine costume with Mary Pickford in Hollywood, 1925

Becker & Maass, Berlin W. 9, phot.

sun shone and closing in the evening. Her costume included four crimson petals, which opened to reveal their golden interior. At the end of the ballet the wired petals were gathered to conceal the dancer still performing bourrées en pointe. As Ashton noted, the lighting was crucial, changing to reflect the time of day and dimming as the petals closed. Without music, colour and lighting, only the skeleton of the production of the ballets remains.

Yet as unsatisfactory as some of the films may appear when first viewed, closer study reveals their importance. The dancer-choreographer Emilyn Claid recorded her reaction when she first saw Pavlova in *The Immortal Swan* in 1978:

> I felt like laughing at first when *Night* did nothing but run and jump landing on the floor, and *Poppy* did nothing but bourrée with her legs in parallel, but then I realised that seen together, these dances showed Pavlova to be an incredibly versatile and physically able person. She had the ability to economize with movement, to be in complete charge of her body, and to be confident in giving out only what was needed to convey her ideas.[4]

Significantly, Pavlova was one of the first ballerinas to take the medium of film seriously, not only allowing herself to be filmed but also recognising the potential of the medium for preserving performance and for teaching and analysing dance. As Maggie Odom Devine has observed, Pavlova was 'the only major classical ballerina of her period to investigate film as a communicative medium for dance':

> Pavlova's interest in filming her repertory was twofold: she viewed the camera as a recording device for herself and her dancers, with the film serving an educative purpose, and she saw film as a potential artistic medium, even though the filming technique of the day largely fell short of her vision.[5]

Pavlova permitted her dances to be recorded on several occasions. She also starred in a feature film, *The Dumb Girl of Portici* (1916), largely to fund her American tour with the Boston Opera Company in 1915–16. Furthermore, she acquired her own movie camera to film life on tour and in the gardens at Ivy House, and in the late 1920s even experimented with recording some of her ballets on stage.

It is interesting to speculate whether Pavlova's involvement with the character dancer, pedagogue and film pioneer Alexander Shiryaev on the first Fazer tour and with her own company in 1911–13 may have encouraged her to take the medium of film more seriously than many of her contemporaries. Shiryaev (1867–1941) had been thwarted in his request to film the Imperial Ballet in St Petersburg, but privately recorded himself and his wife Natalia Matveeva in some of their repertoire; he also created a remarkable range of animated film. The first time we know Pavlova to have appeared on screen was in 1913 in a Berlin studio performing Legat's free-flowing *La Nuit*. The solo, again one in which stage lighting seems to have been particularly significant and which showed off Pavlova's plasticity, was screened at a gala in aid of widows and orphans after she had left the city.

Somewhat disappointed by the results of the recording of *La Nuit*, Pavlova was cautious when approached by producers Wendell Phillips Smalley and Lois Weber to star in *The Dumb Girl of Portici*. It was hardly surprising that as significant a star as Pavlova was asked to appear on the big screen, for in Russia a number of her former colleagues and contemporaries were being drawn into the film industry. It is also possible that Pavlova suggested herself for the mimed role of Fenella, the dumb sister of a revolutionary, since it was one that had been taken by a ballerina since the creation of Auber's opera (also known as *Masaniello*). As she said in an unidentified press interview, 'I stipulated that if I did consent to make a screen debut, it would have to be as the dumb girl of Portici'.

Californian Poppy, one of the solos Pavlova had filmed

Above:
Pavlova with her
dressers on the set
of *The Dumb Girl of Portici*

Left:
Pavlova as Fenella being
thrown into prison in
a still from the film

I began to feel somewhat nervous and apprehensive as to how I should
look in pictures. So I bought a camera and spent some of my idle time in
the country, where I had some of the members of my company take
photographs of me in different poses. Some of these were quite satis-
factory; some were quite otherwise.[6]

The confusing and melodramatic plot of *The Dumb Girl of Portici* was inspired
by the Neapolitan uprising against Spanish oppressors in 1647. It concerns
Fenella, a poor Italian girl who falls in love with and is then betrayed by
a Spanish nobleman disguised as a fisherman, but their affair triggers a
revolution and a national catastrophe. There are some clear parallels with Act I
of *Giselle*, for in *The Dumb Girl of Portici* an innocent girl falls for the elder son
of the Spanish Viceroy, a nobleman in disguise. Like Albrecht in *Giselle*,
Alphonso is already betrothed to a noblewoman. Fenella goes through a variety
of emotions, from joy as she dances on the beach to terror when imprisoned in
a rat-infested cell. Dance plays only a small part in the film and Pavlova's
company makes just two cameo appearances.

In *The Dumb Girl of Portici* Pavlova is an actress rather than a ballerina, and,
as David Vaughan noted, she is appropriately different from other actresses:

Pavlova had learned from Fokine, and perhaps from her own experience,
about what he called 'the mimetic of the whole body'. She realised that
emotion could be expressed from within through the torso, the arms, and
of course the hands, as much as the face ... Not that her face is inexpressive
– throughout, emotions pass across her face in incredibly fast transitions
in a way that few modern actresses would dare to attempt ... yet with
Pavlova is totally believable.[7]

Pavlova made the film over a twelve-week period during the summer of 1915. Initial filming took place in Chicago while the company was dancing at Midway Gardens (an open-air venue) and Pavlova then moved to Universal Studios in Hollywood. The film was directed by the experienced Lois Weber, who also adapted the narrative and co-produced with her husband, Wendell Phillipps Smalley. The original music played to accompany the film was composed by Manuel Klein, who avoided including themes from the opera.

Making *The Dumb Girl of Portici* was a one-off experience for Pavlova, but her dances appear to have been filmed on a number of occasions. It is still uncertain exactly when and where all the dances that survive were recorded and how much footage might still be hidden in archives. The *Dancing Times* in September 1915 reported that *The Swan* had 'been filmed by an enterprising American firm'.[8] Most famously, Pavlova recorded a series of solos at the Pickford-Fairbanks studio on the set of *The Thief of Bagdad*, and at least four others appear to have been made by Lee de Forest in an undecorated space. This filming took place in the mid-1920s during tours in the USA, and newsreel cameras worldwide, including those of the Pathé studios, caught her on stage and at events.

Pavlova was clearly interested in film and in the late 1920s she took two cameras to record her travels and dances. *The Immortal Swan* includes footage of Pavlova in Egypt, India, Java, Australia, South America and Holland.[9] In Australia she tried to film productions using her electrician as cameraman:

She explained with enthusiasm to the Company that by means of her films they would be able to see themselves as the audience saw them. Accordingly the Company spent a week having three ballets filmed

Above:
Invitation to the Dance, one of the ballets Pavlova filmed in Australia in 1929, showing the revised production with sets by Nicolas Benois and costumes by Barbier

Left:
Still from *The Dumb Girl of Portici*

On the set of
The Dumb Girl of Portici.
Behind Pavlova and the goat is the
interior of her cottage (page 128)
with the painted landscape of the
bay of Naples beyond

(*Don Quixote, Invitation to the Waltz, The Fairy Doll*). These were not film-studio performances, but ordinary performances in a theatre, with the camera in the dress circle. It was pointed out to Madame that the lighting was not of sufficient candle-power. 'Never mind,' she said, 'we'll get more lighting! Just let us try and see!'[10]

It is interesting to speculate what Pavlova might have achieved in developing the art of dance on screen, had she lived longer; certainly film appears to have become one of her few real hobbies.

After Pavlova's death Victor Dandré supervised footage being pieced together into an hour-long documentary, *The Immortal Swan*, directed and edited by Edward Nakhimoff and narrated by Aubrey Hitchins. It includes eleven of Pavlova's company performing a *Prélude* from *Chopiniana* (and at the end being joined by children for a *Homage to Anna Pavlova*). It includes discussion of her career illustrated by photographs, footage from her travels and at Ivy House, and glimpses of eleven of her productions. Since *The Immortal Swan*, footage from the Pickford-Fairbanks shoot has been edited into films in London in 1954 by Peter Brinson with music supervised by Leighton Lucas, and in New York in 1964 when pianist Arthur Kleiner made *Anna Pavlova 1882–1931* using a similar selection of material.

While the importance of Pavlova on screen is sometimes played down, and former company members even declared that she did not approve of her films or wish the public to see them, her constant return to filming ballets – even recording *Rondino* in slow motion – suggests a fascination with a medium far too significant to ignore.

Seeing Pavlova on screen can be a frustrating experience. Film performances encourage analysis in a way that live performances do not, and viewers expect to be stunned by the technique of a great ballerina. But Pavlova's artistry never focused on technique, or as her partner Laurent Novikoff wrote, 'Pavlova never adopted mere virtuosity of the dance as her goal... She never deviated from her original purity and her ideas of romantic idealism.' Her performances were always given in response to place, mood, music; technique was something for studio and class, not to be revealed on stage or, indeed, on film. Through her own presentations, as Novikoff continued, Pavlova 'became the symbol of Ballet.'[11]

1   'Pavlova On The Film', *The Manchester Guardian*, 24 October 1916, p. 12.
2   Kathleen Crofton, 'Some Early Ballet Films', *Dancing Times*, July 1954, p. 606.
3   Ashton in *Omnibus: Anna Pavlova (1881–1931)*, produced by Margaret Dale and first transmitted by the BBC on 25 January 1970.
4   Emilyn Claid, 'Dance and Film: The Immortal Swan', *New Dance* 8, Autumn 1978, pp. 10–11.
5   Maggie Odom Devine, 'The Swan Immortalized', *Ballet Review*, Summer 1993, pp. 67–80.
6   Margot Fonteyn, *Pavlova Impressions* (London: Weidenfeld, 1984), p. 87.
7   David Vaughan, 'Theatre Street Revisited, Pavlova Encountered', *Ballet Review* 6:3, 1977–1978, p. 95.
8   The Sitter Out, *Dancing Times*, September 1915, p. 378.
9   These are the locations identified in the programme for *The Immortal Swan*.
10 Walford Hyden, *Pavlova: The Genius of Dance* (London: Constable, 1931), p. 97.
11 Laurent Novikov [*sic*], 'A partner in Praise', in A.H. Franks (ed.), *Pavlova: A Biography* (London: Burke, 1956), p. 96.

Above:
Edmund Nakhimoff, director of
The Immortal Swan, with the corps de
ballet who perform an extract of Clustine's
Chopiniana at the opening of the film, and
Algeranoff who arranged it, 1935

On a carousel with Betty Bolton, who
presented Pavlova with a bouquet when
she opened 'Riverside Revel', a charity fête
at Kew in aid of the West London Hospital,
recorded on newsreel film

PAVLOVA'S LEGACY

Pavlova visiting the Laura Knight
exhibition in 1920; behind her are
Knight's paintings of Pavlova taking
a curtain call after *Autumn Leaves*,
and her company in *The Magic Flute*

The original display of costumes
and memorabilia at the Museum
of London in the 1930s, including
costumes for the *Russian Dance*,
Christmas and *The Swan*

"As a result of her endless tours round the globe and the excitement generated by her own performances Pavlova gave ballet a much stronger identity in the international theatre world"

The name of Anna Pavlova continues to resonate widely, and even for those with no interest in ballet it instantly conjures up the image of a ballerina dressed in a white tutu performing *The Swan*. Just what makes a handful of stars and celebrities so perpetually iconic is hard to say. It seems they have a lasting charisma that transcends the techniques they have mastered, and they become emblematic of the art they represent.

Pavlova has been the subject of numerous books, films, merchandise, performances and exhibitions. She was drawn, painted and sculpted by many artists including Léon Bakst, Maurice Charpentier-Mio, Boris Frödman-Cluzel, Malvina Hoffman, Alexandre Jacovleff, Laura Knight, John Lavery, Ernst Oppler and Savely Sorin. On vacations she sculpted small dancing figures of herself that were later produced in porcelain. Sculptors continue to produce images of her. Two years ago one of Tom Merrifield's life-size statues of Pavlova as the Dragonfly was unveiled at Ivy House, and recently the gilded statue of Pavlova was remade to perch on the cupola of the Victoria Palace in London.[1]

Photographs and films of Pavlova encapsulate the image of what a ballerina should look like. The slim elegant woman with her hair drawn back in a low bun became an iconic image for the twentieth century. She was not entirely alone as there were other notable dancers of her era who also conveyed a sense of modernity – the exotic Ida Rubinstein, the boyish Alice Nikitina, and the tall, leggy Felia Doubrovska – but Pavlova was far more widely known than her colleagues.

Pavlova died of pleurisy in The Hague on 23 January 1931. She had been taken ill in Paris after a Christmas holiday in Monte Carlo, but typically would not let that stand in the way of the start of a new European tour. Her coffin was

Exhibition in 1934 at the Archives de
la danse, Paris, including costumes
for *Bacchanale* and *Au Bal*

transported to London to lie 'in state' at the Russian Orthodox Church, Buckingham Palace Road. After the funeral on 29 January the cortège made its way to Golders Green Crematorium, pausing at Ivy House as it went. A marble urn containing her ashes remains at the crematorium in spite of campaigns by Russians (particularly in 1993) to have them repatriated. Dandré's report on Pavlova's last days, which he distributed to friends and former company members who sent letters of condolence, finished by explaining that he had decided in favour of cremation as, 'if at some future time, Russia should become settled again, and there should be reason for Madame to rest in her native land, to which she was so deeply attached, it will be easy to remove her ashes there'.[2]

Dandré did what he could to keep Pavlova's name in the public eye, publishing a book – *Anna Pavlova, In Art and Life* – in 1932, producing the film *The Immortal Swan* and establishing a memorial service held annually at the Russian Church on 23 January. After Dandré's death in 1944 the service was organised and paid for by Pavlova's wardrobe mistress and friend Mme Manya and subsequently by the Pavlova Society. The service in 1976, one of the last at which a number of 'Pavlova's girls' were present, was filmed for the television series presented by Margot Fonteyn on the history of ballet, *The Magic of the Dance*. In recent years the London Ballet Circle took over the responsibility of ensuring that Pavlova's name was included among those prayed for in the intercessions of the Sunday service closest to 23 January.

Although many of Pavlova's possessions were auctioned, Dandré gave a selection of her costumes and ephemera to the Museum of London and for many years, while the museum was still at Kensington Palace, the collection was on permanent display, although now it is displayed more selectively to prevent fading and deterioration. In 1956 and 1981 the museum mounted special Pavlova exhibitions and organised a series of connected presentations. In 2012 images of the entire Pavlova collection will be available online.

Exhibitions have been held in many countries. The twenty-fifth anniversary of Pavlova's death in 1956 was marked in America and France as well as Britain. In Britain there was also a midnight gala at the Stoll, Kingsway, formerly the London Opera House, where Pavlova had danced in 1913. Parallel celebrations were held in New York with American-based 'Pavlova's girls' assisting in the planning, just as the British-based ones did in Britain. Twenty-five years later, in 1981, Pavlova was commemorated in exhibitions at the Museum of London, and at the California Palace of the Legion of Honor Fine Arts Museum, San Francisco (for which the museum's own holdings were combined with material from the Bancroft Library of the University of California and the Malvina Hoffman Estate).

Between 1974 and 1990 the Anna Pavlova Memorial Museum was established at Ivy House, lovingly created in an upstairs room (but open only on Saturday afternoons) by John and Roberta Lazzarini, founders of the Pavlova Society and authors of two superb and insightful illustrated books. A year after Leonard Newman and Geoffrey Whitlock took over as co-curators of the museum, they presented a Pavlova Festival with support from the London Borough of Barnet. The Lazzarinis secured material for the museum from Mme Manya and drew on their own extensive collection. They also borrowed Pavlova's furniture from Dame

Alicia Markova, which included the dancer's white wooden chairs brought over from Russia and the dressing table from her specially refurbished dressing room at the Palace, which on her death Markova bequeathed to the White Lodge Museum & Ballet Resource Centre.

Pavlova's death coincided with the start of a new European tour for her company. Although several performances had had to be cancelled when Pavlova had been indisposed, her death did not stop the tour from opening in The Hague. Famously on that occasion, and at the performances in London by the Camargo Society at the Apollo Theatre on 25 and 26 January, a spotlight picked out the pattern of *The Swan* on an empty stage. The company in one form or another struggled on for a brief period, appearing at the London Coliseum and elsewhere, but it soon melted away. One of the last times the dancers came together to perform under their shared identity as 'Pavlova's girls' was when Anna Pruzina arranged for eleven of them to perform the adaptation of *Chopiniana* for the opening of *The Immortal Swan*.

Dandré found opportunities to help other ballet companies. He organised an international tour to South Africa, Singapore, Java, Australia, Ceylon, India and Egypt in 1934–35 with the Georgian-born, Paris-based impresario Alexander Lévitoff; Harcourt Algeranoff, one of several dancers in the group who had been with Pavlova, described it as the 'happiest tour I have ever known'.[3] The repertoire was largely that danced by Pavlova's company. The South African leg was led by Vera Nemchinova and Anatole Oboukhoff; in the Far East Olga Spessivtseva and Anatole Vilzak took over. It was unfortunate for Dandré that the Australian tour coincided with the start of Spessivtseva's breakdown, leaving Natasha Bojkovich as ballerina, but he handled this tour as he had Pavlova's – efficiently and with flexibility. It is also certain that he promoted the company as a successor to Pavlova's. As Michelle Potter, historian of the tour, observed, 'It was probably the name Pavlova rather than the concept of classical ballet that was the draw card for audiences', particularly in places that had seen little other ballet since Pavlova's visits.[4] Dandré's experience in running touring ballet companies was also called on in the late 1930s by Colonel de Basil's Ballet Russe, then operating under the names of the Covent Garden Russian Ballet and the Original Ballet Russe.

Former pupils of Pavlova and members of her company contributed to the development of dance in a number of ways: continuing to dance, establishing their own companies or teaching the next generations of dancers. It is impossible to list all those who continued to serve dance but they include the Pole Edvard Borovansky (in Pavlova's company 1926–29), who established an important company bearing his name in Australia which may be regarded as a precursor to the Australian Ballet; Ruth Page who joined Pavlova in South America and Mexico (1918–19) and was responsible for ballet companies in Chicago; Molly Lake, who ran the Ballet Guild which emerged from the Arts Theatre Ballet in Britain during the Second World War and who co-founded the Embassy Ballet; and Mary Skeaping (1925 and 1930) who directed the Royal Swedish Ballet between 1953 and 1962). Skeaping developed a fascination for dance history inspired by her experience of dancing in Pavlova's *Giselle*. She embarked on a project to restore as closely as possible the original 1842 Parisian production; the version she staged in 1971 is still danced by the English National Ballet.

Pavlova in *Christmas* in Berlin, 1924,
with F. Varinski, Alexis Dolinoff,
Alexander Volinine,
D. Domyslawski, J. Zalewski

The roll call of teachers who emerged from Pavlova's company is even longer and includes Pavlova's partners Novikoff and Volinine (an important teacher of male dancers in Paris) and Pierre Vladimirov, who joined the faculty of the School of American Ballet in New York. Among the women who went on to teach were Hilda Butsova, Kathleen Crofton, Cleo Nordi, Anna Pruzina and Muriel Stuart.

A further unsung, but nevertheless influential, figure to emerge from Pavlova's company was Manya Charchevenikova who contributed to the development of the tutu. Mme Manya, as she was always known, became Pavlova's costume maker and personal dresser from the time of her early seasons in London. After Pavlova's death she was persuaded to make tutus for the young ballerina Alicia Markova.

'For Manya, making a costume meant seeing the whole ensemble through. She hand-painted designs, hand-sewed immaculately, cut, sprayed and dried.'[5] She worked for Markova throughout the 1930s and again on her return to Britain after spending the war years in America. Manya's tutus for Markova became particularly important as they were studied by the wardrobe department of the Vic-Wells Ballet and became the template in Britain. The tutu, like all costumes, has continued to develop, but the important contribution by Manya and other British tutu-makers deserves to be acknowledged.

Just as seeing *The Sleeping Beauty* way back in 1890 had inspired Pavlova to become a ballerina, so seeing Pavlova dance was an inspiration for many, from Agnes de Mille in the USA to Robert Helpmann in Australia. Pavlova was a catalyst for those who wanted to dance, because for her dance seemed so personal, so real. In Peru she also inspired Frederick Ashton, who after seeing Pavlova in Lima in 1917 claimed to have been 'injected with the poison'.[6] For Ashton, Pavlova was 'the greatest theatrical genius' he ever saw, and recollections of her performances, in Britain as well as South America, enriched his ballets. From the time he choreographed dances in *Marriage à la Mode* (1930) for Alicia Markova at the Lyric Hammersmith in 1930, he choreographically 'signed' most of his ballets with a combination from the *Gavotte Pavlova*,[7] now popularly known as 'the Fred Step'. He inspired his ballerinas by drawing on his recollection of how Pavlova ran, how she performed her arabesques, and how she used her arms and upper body. The rich *épaulement* in his dances owes much to his constant memory of the great ballerina. Ashton quoted from Pavlova's solos and ballets – *La Nuit* is referenced in the Muses' dance in *Daphnis and Chloë* (1951), appears in choreography for Moira Shearer in the film *The Story of Three Loves* (1952), and reappears for Juliet in the balcony scene from *Romeo and Juliet* (1955). The groups of men surrounding Pavlova in *Invitation to the Dance* and *Christmas* are echoed in the men surrounding Marguerite Gautier (Margot Fonteyn) in *Marguerite and Armand* – a work as much a homage to Pavlova as to Fonteyn.

Another dancer who was inspired and encouraged by Pavlova was Uday Shankar, who arranged the Indian dances in *Oriental Impressions* following Pavlova's 1922–23 tour of the Far East. Shankar was in London to study fine art when a friend introduced him to Pavlova, and he drew on recollections of dances seen in his childhood to choreograph the two purely Indian dances. Although Shankar toured with Pavlova for a season, she would not let him perform in other productions, encouraging him instead to return to India and establish his own company. He maintained that touring with Pavlova taught him the discipline required for dance and how to run a company.

Pavlova changed the way she presented exotic dances, and this too is notable. She may not have entirely escaped the clichés of 'ballet orientalism', but with her two Indian dances in *Oriental Impressions*, and earlier with her presentation of Roshanara's Anglo-Indian dances on her 1912 tour, she took a step towards an authenticity that developed through the twentieth century. The restaging of Pavlova's divertissements presents a challenge as they were so personal to her. *The Swan*, it might be claimed, has simply become universal property, although some dancers endeavour to evoke the spirit of Pavlova in the role. In 1980 Ninette de Valois handed the version she had notated during performances at the Palace to Marguerite Porter who in turn passed it to Marianela Nuñes. Cleo Nordi selectively taught *The Dragonfly* to fleet-footed ballerinas including Nadia Nerina and Marguerite Barbieri. Nerina described the one-and-a-half-minute dance 'as the most tiring solo, apart from *Firebird*, that I ever danced':

> It has masses of little pas de bourrée, very simple and very fast in fifth position, and a great many grand jetés, forward and turning. It never stops except for the few seconds when the dragonfly alights on the ground and plays with its wing... Like other Pavlova solos it looks deceptively simple.[8]

Dancers have also established their own companies to celebrate Anna Pavlova. In America in 1981 two principal dancers, Anne Marie De Angelo and Starr Danias, headed tribute tours. De Angelo's *Tribute to Pavlova* was said to give 'a sprinkling of what made [Pavlova] so special' and divertissements included *Autumn Bacchanale, Le Papillon, Christmas* and *Californian Poppy*. Danias' *The Pavlova Celebration* benefited from Muriel Stuart staging *The Dragonfly* and *The Swan*, Ruth Page mounting *Idylle* and *Polka Pizzicato* and Irina Fokine (Pavlova's goddaughter) *Les Préludes* and *The Fairy Doll*. A decade later in Britain the small company Ballet Creations, established by Ursula Hageli and Richard Slaughter, celebrated the art of Pavlova, assisted in their recreation of Pavlova's repertory by Rita Glynde. Their programmes included *Bacchanale, La Nuit, Gavotte* and *The Fairy Doll*. While performing in the late 1990s they collected recollections from those who saw Pavlova dance, preserving them before they were lost.

Pavlova's image both haunts and inspires choreographers. Choreographing to music Pavlova danced to can be challenging. If using, for example, Saint-Saëns' *Carnival of the Animals*, a choreographer has to choose whether or not to include 'The Swan'. It can, nevertheless, be presented imaginatively, as it was by Siobhan Davies when she created her original version for Philippe Giradoux and Second Stride. The iconography of Pavlova is equally inspirational. When Matthew Bourne created his hugely successful *Swan Lake,* it was Pavlova, with her swan Jack in her lap, who was the source of the eye-catching publicity for the first production.

Since his death in 1929 much has been made of the impact of Diaghilev's Ballets Russes on the subsequent history of dance, while the long-term importance of Anna Pavlova is often overlooked. Dance commentators and historians have a tendency to dismiss the ballerina as conservative, perpetuating old-

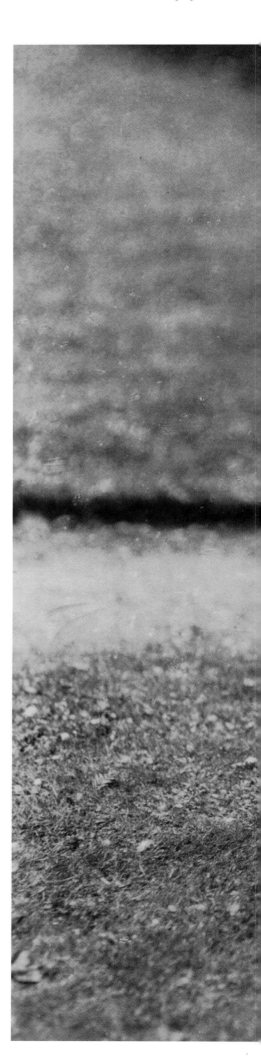

fashioned ballets, while recognising that she was and remains an icon of the dance. The dismissal of Pavlova is curious given that the repertoire of ballets she danced, based on the creations of Marius Petipa and Alexander Gorsky, are those that the ballet public still loves to watch. Pavlova's repertoire includes extracts of the *Paquita, Nutcracker, The Sleeping Beauty, Raymonda* and, from earlier periods, *Giselle* and *La Fille mal gardée*, both filtered through Imperial Ballet productions. Without ignoring the importance of Diaghilev's inclusion of *The Sleeping Beauty/Princess* in London and occasional inclusion of *Swan Lake* in the Ballets Russes repertoire, it is the ballets Pavlova danced that audiences flock to today.

Pavlova undoubtedly left a lasting legacy for twentieth-century dance. She was a woman who took control of her career, who found colleagues to support her projects, and was driven to dance for new audiences, however remote and however challenging the conditions she faced. As a result of her endless tours round the globe and the excitement generated by her own performances, Pavlova gave ballet a much stronger identity in the international theatre world. At the same time, as Frederick Ashton acknowledged, it was 'in London she made her home and inspired so many who were to create the English Ballet'.[9]

1   Pavlova's statue was installed when the Frank Matcham-designed theatre was opened in 1911, but removed in 1939. The current statue to the original design is a replacement.
2   Victor Dandré, 'The Last Days', *Dance Magazine*, August 1931, p. 60.
3   Others were Kathleen Crofton and Molly Lake.
4   Michelle Potter, 'The Dandré-Levitoff Russian Ballet, 1934–1935: Australia and beyond', *Dance Research* 29.1, Summer 2011, p. 85.
5   Maurice Leonard, *Markova: The Legend. The Authorised Biography* (London: Hodder and Stoughton, 1995), p. 145.
6   David Vaughan, *Frederick Ashton and his Ballets* (London: Black, 1977), p. 4.
7   Vaughan in ibid. (p. 9) describes this as 'posé en arabesque, coupé dessous, small développé à la seconde, pas de bourrée dessous, pas de chat'.
8   Clement Crisp (ed.), *Ballerina Portraits and Impressions of Nadia Nerina* (London: Weidenfeld), unpaginated.
9   Frederick Ashton, 'Message from the Patrons', *The 1988 Pavlova Festival* (festival programme, ed. Leonard Newman).

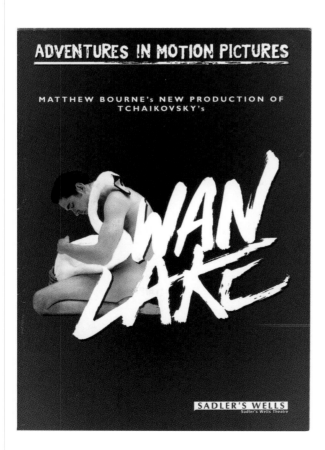

Programme cover for the first performances of Matthew Bourne's *Swan Lake* in 1984, showing the publicity image inspired by iconography of Pavlova with the swan Jack

Above:
As the Dragonfly, one of Pavlova's
solos that is occasionally revived

Left:
With Varinsky in the *Gavotte* in
New Zealand, 1926

Mary Skeaping's *Giselle* with
Galina Samsova in the title role
performed by London Festival
Ballet, 1971; Skeaping's research
into the ballet was inspired by
working with Pavlova at Covent
Garden in 1925

Margot Fonteyn as Marguerite
Gautier surrounded by admirers in
Frederick Ashton's *Marguerite and
Armand* for The Royal Ballet, 1963

Ursula Hageli posed in costume
for *Bacchanale* by the urn in the
grounds at Ivy House to promote
Ballet Creations' programme
Portrait of Pavlova which they
toured throughout Britain in
the 1990s

THE SWAN

In her swan costume in the garden
at Ivy House

63.S. **MADAME ANNA PAVLOVA.** PHOTO
BEAGLES' POSTCARDS. THE CELEBRATED RUSSIAN DANCER. SCHNEIDER.

The Swan

One of Pavlova's costumes for *The Swan*. Her costume-maker Mme Manya claimed 'she never wore her Swan costume more than twice without the skirts of the tutu being renewed'

Anna Pavlova's name will always be associated with the solo *The Swan*, popularly known as *The Dying Swan* and listed in early British tour programmes as *The Passing of the Swan*. The solo is only three minutes long, yet it appears that no one who ever saw Pavlova dance it ever forgot the experience. By the end of her life *The Swan* had become so famous that she was forced to include it in most of her programmes to avoid disappointing her audiences.

Choreographed by Mikhail Fokine to 'Le Cygne' ('The Swan') movement from *The Carnival of the Animals* (1886) by Camille Saint-Saëns, it was performed by the ballerina in a costume designed by Léon Bakst that consisted of a white tutu decorated with swan's wings and a headdress of white feathers framing Pavlova's face. The costume, which was remade on many occasions, recalls the one worn in the four-act ballet *Swan Lake* by Odette, whose own costume, and indeed Odette's complete role, came to be re-interpreted in the context of Fokine's ballet.

The Swan was performed on an undecorated stage, the solo figure picked out by a spotlight. It evokes the music, played on harp (suggesting the rippling of water) and cello, in Saint-Saëns' score. The very choice of accompaniment was innovative in the early twentieth century when it was still rare to use established scores that observed none of the conventions of traditional ballet music. The choreography combined formal classical ballet steps – a sequence of bourrées broken by an occasional attitude – with an expressive, free use of the arms to suggest the beating and fluttering of wings.

In a reminiscence of Pavlova, Victor Dandré's nephew Michel Barroy claimed to have been present when ideas for the solo were first brought together. He was with Pavlova, Fokine and Dandré when they saw swans on a lake near St Petersburg and stopped so that Pavlova, who felt a natural affinity with these birds, could

feed them. Shortly afterwards he noticed Fokine at a benefit concert at which the actor Hodotov presented a 'melodeclamation', a form of dramatic recitation to musical accompaniment, of Konstantin Balmont's poem *The Dying Swan*. The poem describes a still lake on which a wounded swan returns to die.[1]

Fokine described creating the ballet for Pavlova, saying that at the time he was asked to create a solo he had been playing Saint-Saëns' 'Swan' on a mandolin to piano accompaniment:

> The dance was composed in a few minutes. It was almost an improvisation. I demonstrated for her, she directly behind me. Then she danced and I walked alongside of her, curving her arms and directing details of the poses.[2]

Fokine felt that *The Swan* made an important statement about his approach to choreography, for not only had he been accused of rejecting pointe work for women but it was a dance that clearly went beyond technique. It required the dancer to use her entire body, the arms, head and torso as well as the legs, which had been the focus of late nineteenth-century choreography. As Fokine later said, 'This dance aims not so much at the eyes of the spectator, but at his soul, at his emotions.'[3]

The full history of the solo's creation is unclear. Pavlova first danced it at the Maryinsky Theatre, St Petersburg, on 22 December 1907 at a performance in aid of Her Highness Olga Alexandrovna's charity for newborn children and impoverished mothers at the Imperial Maternal Establishment. Yet another ballerina, Lydia Kyasht, makes it clear in her autobiography, *Romantic Recollections*, that she herself gave the work its first performance two years earlier – in 1905 – at the Hall of Nobles for a charity matinee in aid of veterans of the Russo-Japanese War.[4] Kyasht was accompanied on the cello by Berednikoff, the grandson of the Lord Mayor of St Petersburg. It is perfectly possible that

Fokine created two similar works but with different choreographic details so that each ballerina legitimately thought of the solo as her own.

Pavlova gave the ballet a sense of narrative. The swan is first seen gliding peacefully on water as she enters with her back to the audience. In some accounts it is suggested that she is shot by an unseen marksman, the wound indicated by the blood-red jewel on the bodice of some versions of her costume. Gradually she resigns herself to her fate and folding her head under her quivering wings she shudders and dies. Or as early programmes for Pavlova's tour describe it, 'this dance is descriptive of the last death song of a swan':

> In this dance one follows the movements of a swan in perfect harmony with the strains of the music. Gradually the movements of the swan and the music mingle together, and, as the swan falls to earth dead, the music dies away.[5]

Eyewitnesses such as Ninette de Valois, who notated the solo when Pavlova danced it at the Palace Theatre matinees in 1913, observed that the choreography of *The Swan* changed considerably over the 24 years Pavlova danced it.[6] This was hardly surprising given the spontaneity Pavlova brought to her dances, and even the version Pavlova was presenting at the Palace may have already changed from the way she first danced it in St Petersburg.

This solo became such an extraordinary success that it was danced by numerous performers, many creating their own choreography in the style of Fokine's ballet for Pavlova. Children, dancers in variety, and even many later ballerinas have performed their own interpretations. In 1917 the film-maker Evgeni Bauer produced his narrative film *The Dying Swan*, inspired by the ballet, in which Gizella, a deaf-mute dancer (played by Moscow ballerina Vera Karalli), falls into the clutches of a crazed necrophilic artist.

Pavlova made several film recordings of *The Swan* and even Kathleen Crofton acknowledged that 'Pavlova's movements are a revelation here'. For Crofton the film reveals 'the essential mechanics of strength and control of back and hips being applied in great degree in order to allow relaxation above, and therefore complete freedom of expression':

> Her lovely arms seem to breathe as she opens and lifts them. Her whole being is the dance. Hands, arms, shoulders, neck and head appear softly to dissolve from one beautiful position to another; unconventional perhaps, yet entirely classical in feeling. Her unique position in the history of dance is established beyond doubt; it is hers for all time – Pavlova, the incomparable.[7]

1   Michel Barroy, 'Reniniscences of Pavlova', *Dance Magazine*, April 1956, p. 39.
2   Mikhail Fokine, 'Michel Fokine Remembers – Pavlova As She Was in the Beginning', *Dance Magazine,* August 1931, p. 49.
3   Mikhail Fokine, *Fokine: Memoirs of a Ballet Master* (trans. Vitale Fokine; ed. Anatole Chujoy) (London: Constable, 1961), p. 222. Fokine states that the ballet was created at the Hall of the Nobles in 1905. Research to verify the date of Pavlova's first performance was undertaken by Vera Krasovskaya.
4   Lydia Kyasht, *Romantic Recollections* (London: Brentano, 1929), pp. 86–87.
5   Synopsis from programmes for 1912 and 1913 regional tours.
6   Ninette de Valois was researching for her role as Anna Pavlova in Lila Fields' 1913 revue in which her young pupils appeared as famous music-hall artists.
7   Kathleen Crofton, 'Some Early Ballet Films', *Dancing Times*, July 1954, p. 606.

Pavlova made her entry in
The Swan bourréeing with her
back to the audience

ANNA PAVLOVA AND COMPANY PERFORMANCES IN BRITAIN

The following list details Pavlova's public performances in Britain. It excludes galas, private soirées and other events. Unfortunately there is no evidence of show reports surviving for Pavlova's company (which would detail what was danced at each performance) and so the listing is compiled from programmes, advertisements and press reports – never reliable sources – and confirmed by the diaries of participants. This list is as complete as it could be made within the time available and the repertoire of works is indicative of the ballets – but not divertissements – that the company was performing.

Pavlova with Uday Shankar in *Krishna and Radha*

1910

Date	Town	Venue	Notes on programme
18 April – 6 August	London	Palace Theatre	Programme of Divertissements

1911

Date	Town	Venue	Notes on programme
17 April – 2 September	London	Palace Theatre	Programme of divertissements, Chopin dances turned into a suite, *Snowflakes*
24 October – 11 November	London	Royal Opera House	(with Diaghilev's Ballets Russes Pavlova danced in *Le Carnaval, Les Sylphides, Cléopâtre, Giselle, Pavillon d'Armide* and *L'Oiseau d'or*)
13 – 18 November	Newcastle upon Tyne	Theatre Royal	
20 – 25 November	Glasgow	King's Theatre	
27 November – 2 December	Edinburgh	Lyceum	
4 – 9 November	Birmingham	Prince of Wales	
11 – 16 December	Manchester	Theatre Royal	
28 – 30 December	Eastbourne	Devonshire Park Theatre	

1912

Date	Town	Venue	Notes on programme
13 January	Richmond (Surrey)	Richmond Theatre	
22 – 27 January	Dublin	Gaiety Theatre	
29 January – February	Belfast		
26 February – 2 March	Liverpool	Shakespeare Theatre	The 1911-12 Divertissement tour also included playlets *Batchelor's Babies* by Leedham Banstock, *Judged by Appearances* by Frederick Fenn
18 April – 3 August	London	Palace Theatre	Repertoire included Grand pas classique from *Paquita, Amarilla, La Fille mal gardée* and divertissements
9 – 14 September	Harrogate	Kursaal	1912 tour ballets included a suite from
16 – 21 September	Blackpool	Her Majesty's Opera House	*Coppélia Act 1, La Fille mal gardée*
23 – 28 September	Liverpool	Shakespeare Theatre	included playlets *The House that Jack*
30 September – 5 October	Hull	Grand Theatre	*Built* by Albert E. Drinkwater, Roshanara
7 – 12 October	Bristol	Princes Theatre	presented her India dances.
14 – 19 October	Manchester	Theatre Royal	
21 – 26 October	Birmingham	Prince of Wales	
28 October – 2 November	Leeds	Grand	
4 – 9 November	Liverpool	Shakespeare Theatre	
11 – 16 November	Edinburgh	Royal Lyceum	
18 – 23 November	Glasgow	King's Theatre	
25 – 30 November	Newcastle upon Tyne	Tyne Theatre & Opera House	
2 – 7 December	Nottingham	Theatre Royal	
9 – 14 December	Cardiff	New Theatre	

1913

Date	Town	Venue	Notes on programme
21 April – 9 August	London	Palace Theatre	*Les Préludes*, suite from *Coppélia Act I*,
			Invitation to the Dance
1913	London	London Opera House	Repertoire *Giselle, The Magic Flute,*
			Oriental Fantasy, Une Soiree de Chopin and divertissement

1914

Date	Town	Venue	Notes on programme
5 – 6 September	Bournemouth	Winter Gardens	Divertissement programme
12 October	London	Palace Theatre	*Flora's Awakening* and divertissement

1920

Date	Town	Venue	Notes on programme
12 April – 5 June	London	Theatre Royal Drury Lane	Repertoire included *Amarilla, Autumn Leaves, Chopiniana,*
			Flora's Awakening, Giselle, The King's Daughter, Magic Flute,
			Orpheus, La Péri, Les Préludes, Sleeping Beauty (Visions),
			Snowflakes, Thais, Walpurgis Night
7 June	Margate	Winter Gardens	
8 June	Eastbourne	Devonshire Park Theatre	
10 June	Brighton	Brighton Palace Pier	
11 June	Southsea	South Parade Pier	
12 June	Kingston		Divertissement tour
15 June – 10 July	London	Princes Theatre	Repertoire included *Amarilla, Chopiniana, The Fairy Doll,*
			Flora's Awakening, Invitation to the Dance, The King's Daughter,
			Mexican Dances, La Péri, Walpurgis Night, Sleeping Beauty
23 – 24 July	Southend	Arcadia	
26 – 27 July	Bournemouth	Winter Garden	
28 – 29 July	Bristol	Hippodrome	
30 – 31 July	Bath	Theatre Royal	
25 August	Manchester	Hipppodrome	
10 – 11 September	Liverpool	Olympia	

1921

Date	Town	Venue	Notes on programme
27 June – 10 July	London	Queens Hall	*Chopiniana* and divertissement
15 July	Southsea	South Parade Pier	
20 July	Bath	Theatre Royal	
21 July	Bristol	Colston Hall	
22 July	Weston-super-Mare	Grand Pier Pavilion	
23 July	Plymouth	Palace	
25 July	Torquay	Pavilion	
28 July	Newquay	Pavilion	
6 August	Nottingham	Empire	
24 August	Sheffield	Empire	
25 August	Newcastle upon Tyne	Empire	
26 – 27 August	Harrogate	Royal Hall	Tour repertoire included *Chopiniana, Mexican Dances*
			and divertissements
29 August – 3 September	Blackpool	Her Majesty's Opera House	
5 – 10 September	Liverpool	Olympia Theatre	
12 – 17 September	Glasgow	Alhambra Theatre	
19 – 24 September	Edinburgh	King's Theatre	Tour repertoire included *The Magic Flute,*
			Snowflakes and divertissements

1923

Date	Town	Venue	Notes on programme
16 July	Leicester	De Montfort Hall	
17 July	Nottingham	Empire	

1923 (cont.)

Date	Town	Venue	Notes on programme
18 July	Chesterfield	Corporation Theatre	
18 July	Mansfield	Y.M.C.A	
19 July	Derby	Hippodrome	
20 July	Sheffield	Empire	
21 July	Bradford	Alhambra	
23 July	Harrogate	Royal Hall	
24 July	Scarborough	Floral Hall	
25 – 26 July	Manchester	Palace	
27 July	Huddersfield	Theatre Royal	
28 July	Hull	Palace	
30 July	Reading	County Theatre	
31 July	Margate	Winter Garden	
1 August	Eastbourne	Devonshire Park Theatre	
2 August	Hastings	Elite Theatre	
3 – 4 August	Bournemouth	Winter Garden	
6 August	Cheltenham	Town hall	
7 August	Cardiff	Empire	
8 August	Swansea	Empire	
9 August	Malvern	Assembly Rooms	
10 August	Colwyn Bay	Pier Pavilion	
11 August	Leeds	Empire	
13 August	Newcastle upon Tyne	Empire	
14 – 15 August	Glasgow	Alhambra	
16 – 17 August	Edinburgh		
18 August	Liverpool	Empire	Tour repertoire included *Egyptian Dances* and divertissements
10 – 22 September	London	Royal Opera House	Repertoire included *Ajanta's Frescoes, Amarilla, Chopiniana, Dionysus, The Fairy Doll, La Fille mal gardée, The Magic Flute, Old Russian Folk Lore (Russian Fairy Tale), Oriental Impressions, Polish Wedding* and divertissements

1924

Date	Town	Venue	Notes on programme
8 September – 4 October	London	Royal Opera House	Repertoire included *Ajanta's Frescoes, Amarilla, Autumn Leaves, Chopiniana, Coppélia Act 1, Don Quixote, The Fairy Doll, Flora's Awakening, Visions, Invitation to the Dance, The Magic Flute, Old Russian Folk Lore, Oriental Impressions, Polish Wedding, Les Préludes, The Romance of the Mummy, Snowflakes* and divertissements

1925

Date	Town	Venue	Notes on programme
22 September	Margate	Winter Gardens	
28 September – 24 October	London	Royal Opera House	Repertoire included *Ajanta's Frescoes, Amarilla, Autumn Leaves, Chopiniana, Coppélia Act 1, Don Quixote, The Fairy Doll, La Fille mal gardée, Giselle, Invitation to the Dance, The Magic Flute, Old Russian Folk Lore, Oriental Impressions, Polish Wedding, Visions, Romance of the Mummy, Snowflakes* and Divertissement
26 October	Leicester	De Montfort Hall	
27 October	Northampton	New Theatre	
28 October	Buxton	Royal Opera House	
29 – 30 October	Manchester	Hippodrome	
31 October	Bradford	Alhambra	
2 November	Edinburgh	Usher Hall	
3 November	Dundee	Caird Hall	
4 November	Aberdeen	Music Hall	
5 – 6 November	Glasgow	St Andrews Hall	
7 November	Newcastle upon Tyne	Empire	
9 November	Leeds	Empire	
10 – 11 November	Birmingham	Grand Theatre	
12 November	Cardiff	Winter Garden	
16 November	Bristol	Colston Hall	
17 November	Torquay	Pavilion	Tour repertoire included *Chopiniana* and divertissements

Pavlova in Bombay, 1923

1927

Date	Town	Venue	Notes on programme
12 – 24 September	London	Royal Opera House	Repertoire included *Amarilla, Autumn Leaves, Chopiniana,*
			Coppélia Act I, *Don Quixote, The Fairy Doll, La Fille mal gardée,*
			Magic Flute, Snowflakes and divertissements
3 October	Margate	Winter Garden	
4 October	Folkestone	Leas Cliff Pavilion	
5 October	Hastings	White Rock Pavilion	
6 October	Brighton	Hippodrome	
6 October	Eastbourne	Devonshire Park Theatre	
7 October	Shanklin	Pier Casino	
8 October	Bournemouth	Winter Gardens	
10 October	Leicester	De Montfort Hall	
11 October	Nottingham	Empire	
12 October	Derby	Hippodrome	
13 October	Sheffield	Hippodrome	
14 October	Leeds	Town Hall	
14 October	Halifax	Theatre Royal	
17 October	Huddersfield	Town Hall	
18 October	Bradford	King's Hall	
19 October	Blackburn	King George's Hall	
20 October	Llandudno	Pier Pavilion	
21 October	Shrewsbury	Empire	
22 October	Hanley	Victoria Hall	
24 October	Manchester	Free Trade Hall	
25 October	Warrington	Parr Hall	
26 October	Manchester	Free Trade Hall	
27 – 28 October	Liverpool	Philharmonic Hall	
29 October	Preston	Public Hall	
31 October – 5 November	Birmingham	Theatre Royal	
7 – 8 November	Glasgow	St. Andrews Hall	
9 November	Dundee	Caird Hall	
10 November	Aberdeen	Music Hall	
11 November	Perth	City Hall	
12 November	Edinburgh	The Usher Hall	
14 November	Newcastle upon Tyne	Palace Theatre	
15 November	Middlesbrough	Town Hall	
16 November	West Hartlepool	Town Hall	
17 November	Darlington	Hippodrome	
18 November	York	Empire	
18 November	Scarborough	Futurist Theatre	
19 November	Hull	City Hall	
21 November	Newark	Palace Theatre	
22 November	Oxford	Town Hall	
24 November	Reading	Town Hall	
25 November	Portsmouth	Guild Hall	
26 November	Bournemouth	Winter Garden	
28 November	Bristol	Colston Hall	
29 November	Cardiff	Empire	
30 November	Swansea	Empire	
1 December	Plymouth	Guild Hall	
2 December	Torquay	Pavilion	
3 December	Exeter	Civic Hall	
5 December	Bath	Assembly Rooms	
6 December	Cheltenham	Town Hall	
7 December	Buxton	Opera House	
8 December	Kidderminster	Opera House	
9 December	Worcester	Public Hall	
10 December	Rugby	Prince of Wales Theatre	Tour includes *Chopiniana* and divertissements
			except for the week in Birmingham when
			The Fairy Doll and *Amarilla* were included

1929

Date	Town	Venue	Notes on programme
2 – 7 December	Golders Green	Hippodrome	At Golders Green: *The Fairy Doll, La Fille mal gardée, Visions,*
9 – 14 December	Streatham	Streatham Hill Theatre	*Walpurgis Night.* At Streatham: *Invitation to the Dance, The Magic*
16 – 21 December	Brighton	Hippodrome	*Flute, Polish Wedding, Snowflakes, Autumn Leaves.* The tour repertoire
			drew on these works and divertissements

1930

Date	Town	Venue	Notes on programme
8 – 13 September	Southampton	Empire	At most venues on this tour the first four performances included
15 – 20 September	Streatham	Streatham Hill Theatre	*Autumn Leaves, Polish Wedding, Invitation to the Dance* and
22 – 27 September	Cardiff	Empire	divertissements; the second four *Amarilla, Venusberg*
29 September – 4 October	Bristol	Prince's Theatre	and divertissements. At Streatham and Bradford the first half of the
6 – 11 October	Birmingham	Prince of Wales Theatre	week was *The Fairy Doll, Chopiniana* and divertissements
13 – 18 October	Leeds	Royal Theatre	
20 – 25 October	Bradford	Alhambra Theatre	
27 October – 1 November	Manchester	Palace Theatre	
3 – 8 November	Liverpool	Empire Theatre	
10 – 15 November	Sheffield	Empire Theatre	
17 – 22 November	Glasgow	Alhambra Theatre	
24 – 29 November	Edinburgh	Empire Theatre	

1930 (cont.)

Date	Town	Venue	Notes on programme
1 December	Dundee	Caird Hall	Divertissement programmes
2 December	Newcastle upon Tyne	City Hall	
3 December	Halifax	Victoria Hall	
4 December	Leicester	De Montfort Hall	
5 December	Hanley	Victoria Hall	
6 December	Preston	Public Hall	
8 – 13 December	Golders Green	Hippodrome	

The ballets performed during the last week of Pavlova's performing career were *Autumn Leaves, Invitation to the Dance, Polish Wedding* and *Amarilla, Venusberg* and the *Grand pas classique* from *Paquita*, both programmes with divertissements

At Salzo-Maggiore she met up with her friend, the artist Alexander Jacovleff

BIBLIOGRAPHY

Pavlova on holiday at Salzo-Maggiore

Algeranoff, Harcourt, *My Years with Pavlova*
(London: Heinemann, 1957)

Anna Pavlova, St Petersburg State Museum of
Theatre and Music (St Petersburg: Art Deco, 2007)

Applin, Arthur, *The Stories of the Russian Ballet*
(London: Everett, 1911)

Barbier, Georges, *25 Costumes pour le théâtre*
(Paris: Bloch & Meynial, 1927)

Barroy, Michel, 'Reminiscences of Pavlova',
Dance Magazine (April 1956), pp. 39, 81

Beaumont, Cyril W., *Anna Pavlova*
(London: Beaumont, 1932)

_____, *Michel Fokine and his Ballets*
(London: Beaumont, 1935)

_____, *The Diaghilev Ballet in London*
(London: Putnam, 1940)

Bedells, Phyllis, *My Dancing Days*
(London: Phoenix House, 1954)

Benari, Naomi, *Vagabonds and Strolling Dancers:
The Lives and Times of Molly Lake and Travis Kemp*
(London: Imperial Society of Teachers of Dancing,
[1990])

Betjeman, John, 'Ballet-Goer's London Guide 4',
Ballet 12:1 (March 1952), p. 33

Beumers, Birgit, Bocharov, Victor, and Robinson,
David (eds.), *Alexander Shiryaev: Master of Movement*
(Pordonone: Le Giornate del Cinema Muto, 2009)

Chaplin, Charlie *My Autobiography* (London: Bodley
Head, 1964) Claid, Emilyn, 'Dance and Film:
The Immortal Swan', *New Dance* 8 (Autumn 1978),
pp. 10–11

Clarke, Mary, *Six Great Dancers*
(London: Hamish Hamilton, 1957)

Crisp, Clement (ed.), *Ballerina Portraits and
Impressions of Nadia Nerina* (London: Weidenfeld,
[1978])

Curnock, Grace, 'Madame Pavlova, Making Final
Preparations for Her Coming Tour', *Daily Mail*,
2 November 1911, p. 4

Dandré, Victor, *Anna Pavlova, In Art and Life*
(London: Cassell, [1932])

Devine, Maggie Odom, 'The Swan Immortalized',
Ballet Review (Summer 1993), pp. 67–80

Fokine, Mikhail, 'Michel Fokine Remembers –
Pavlova As She Was in the Beginning', *Dance
Magazine* (August 1931), pp. 11–49

Fokine, Vitale, *Fokine, Memoirs of a Ballet Master*
(ed. Anatole Chujoy) (London: Constable, 1961)

Folkard & Hayward (auctioneers), *Ivy House
Hampstead Heath* (London 1931)

Franks, A. H. (ed.), *Anna Pavlova*
(London: Burke, 1956)

Haskell, Arnold, et al., *Anna Pavlova 1882–1931:
Catalogue of the Commemorative Exhibition organised
by the London Museum in association with the Anna
Pavlova Memorial Committee* (London: London
Museum, 1956)

Horosko, Marian, 'In the Shadow of Russian
Tradition: Hilda Butsova', *Dance Magazine*
(November 1972), pp. 64–69

_____, 'Pavlova and Muriel Stuart,
Dance Magazine (January 1976), pp. 63–64

Hurok, Sol, *Impresario* (ed. Ruth Goode) (London:
Macdonald, 1947)

Hyden, Walford, *Pavlova: the Genius of Dance*
(London: Constable, 1931)

Ilyin, Eugene K., 'Memories of Anna Pavlova', *World
Review* (December 1949), pp. 37–41, 78

Johnson, A. E., *The Russian Ballet*
(London: Constable, 1913)

Kerensky, Oleg, *Anna Pavlova*
(London: Hamish Hamilton, 1973)

Knight, Laura, *Oil Paint and Grease Paint*
(London: Nicholson & Watson, 1936)

Kschessinskaya, Mathilde, *Dancing in St Petersburg:
The Memoirs of Kschessinska* (trans. Arnold Haskell)
(London: Gollancz, 1960)

Kyasht, Lydia, *Romantic Recollections* (ed. Erica Beale)
(London: Brentano, 1929)

Laakkonen, Johanna, *Canon and Beyond. Edvard Fazer
and the Imperial Russian Ballet 1908–1910* (Helsinki:
Academia Scientiarum Fennica, 2009)

Lake, Molly, 'I remember Pavlova', *Dance and
Dancers* (December 1956), p. 12

Lazzarini, John and Roberta, *Pavlova: Repertoire
of a Legend* (London: Collier MacMillan, 1980)

_____ (eds.),
Pavlova: Impressions. Presented by Margot Fonteyn
(London: Weidenfeld, 1984)

Legat, Nicolas, 'As Friends Recall Her',
Dancing Magazines (August 1931), p. 21

Leonard, Maurice, *Markova: The Legend.
The authorised biography* (London: Hodder and
Stoughton, 1995)

Lifar, Serge, *The Three Graces: Anna Pavlova, Tamara
Karsavina, Olga Spessivtseva. The Legends and the
Truth* (London: Cassell, 1959)

MacDonald, Nesta, *Diaghilev Observed by the Critics
in England and the United States 1911–1929* (London:
Dance Books, 1975)

Mackrell, Judith, *Bloomsbury Ballerina*
(London: Phoenix, 2009)

Magriel, Paul, *Pavlova* (London: Black, 1945)

Manya [Charchevnickova], 'A Perfectionist in
Everything', *Dance and Dancers* (January 1956), p. 16

Money, Keith, *Anna Pavlova: her Life and Art*
(New York: Knoff, 1982)

Nectoux, Jean-Michel, *1913: Le Théâtre des Champs-
Élysées Paris* (Paris: Éditions de la Réunion des
musées nationaux, 1987)

Newman, Leonard, *Ivy House: A brief history of the
house made world famous as the home of the legendary
ballet dancer Anna Pavlova* (London: Newman, 1992)
(privately circulated)

Oukrainsky, Serge, *My Two Years with Anna Pavlova*
(New York: Sutton House, 1940)

Palatsky, Eugene, 'Pavlova, Rediscovered!',
Dance Magazine (December 1964), pp. 34–36

Potter, Michelle, 'The Dandré-Levitoff Russian
Ballet, 1934–1935: Australia and beyond',
Dance Research 29:1 (Summer 2011), pp. 61-96

Richardson, P. S. J., 'Pavlova: Some Memories',
Dancing Times (February 1931), p. 690

Rogers, Quentin, and Crofton, Kathleen, 'Some
Early Ballet Films', *Dancing Times* (July 1954), p. 606

Sitter Out (The), *Dancing Times* (September 1915),
p. 378

Sokolova, Lydia, *Dancing for Diaghilev:
the Memoirs of Lydia Sokolova* (ed. Richard Buckle)
(London: John Murray, 1960)

Stier, Theodore, *With Pavlova round the World*
(London: Hurst & Blackell, [1927])

Stuart, Muriel, 'Studio Recollections',
Dance Magazine (August 1932), pp. 12, 60

Svetlov, Valerian, *Anna Pavlova* (London: British
Continental, 1931)

Trukhanova, Natalia [*sic*], 'Anna Pavlova,
a remembrance' (trans. All Klimov and Alison
Hilton), *Dance Magazine* (January 1976), pp. 44–50

Valois, Ninette de, *Come Dance with Me: A Memoir
1898–1956* (London: Hamish Hamilton, 1957)

Vaughan, David, 'Further Annals of
The Sleeping Beauty: Anna Pavlova, 1916',
Ballet Review 3:2 (1969), pp. 3–18

_____, *Frederick Ashton and his Ballets*
(London: Black, 1977)

_____, 'Theatre Street Revisited,
Pavlova Encountered',
Ballet Review 6:3 (1977–1978), pp. 90–96

ACKNOWLEDGEMENTS

Pavlova preparing her shoes in her apartment in St Petersburg

The idea for *Pavlova*: *Twentieth-Century Ballerina* came from Irene Newton, Cultural Programmer at the London Jewish Cultural Centre, Ivy House, and Artistic Director of 'Pavlova 2012', who was determined that the centenary of Pavlova's acquisition of Ivy House should be marked. As a result the book is not a biography but a celebration of facets of Pavlova's life as an inspirational dancer, an independent career woman and megastar loved by the media and her audiences throughout the world. The book focuses primarily on Pavlova's contribution to the developing dance scene in Britain while being entirely aware that this was not her full story.

There are many people to thank for making this book possible, most notably Anya Sainsbury and Cathy Giangrande who worked tirelessly to secure funding.

For illustrations and research we have drawn on a number of sources. The Museum of London holds a particularly rich collection of material – indicative of Pavlova's importance for the metropolis. Caroline Hamilton worked closely with the staff of the photographic, ephemera and costume collections at the Museum and our particular thanks go to Hilary Davidson and Sean Waterman. Caroline also used the Selfridge Archive in London and, while in Australia, also undertook research at the Arts Centre, Melbourne, and the National Library of Australia; our thanks go to the staff at all these collections.

In Britain we would like to thank the White Lodge Museum & Ballet Resource Centre and in particular Anna Meadmore and Edward Small, as well as the staff of the British Library Reading Rooms at Kings Cross and Colindale.

I must thank my colleagues at the Victoria and Albert Museum and in particular Amy King and Thea Stevenson in the Theatre & Performance Department, Ken Jackson and the photographic team and Olivia Stroud in V&A Images.

Many friends, scholars and collectors have been particularly helpful, including Noel Essex, Andrew Foster, Bernard Horrocks, Ursula Hageli, Roberta Lazzarini, Leonard Newman, Helen Ordish (whose collection featured on *The Antiques Roadshow*), Mary Pritchard, David Robinson and David Vaughan, as well as private collectors who wish to remain anonymous. We would like to thank the photographers, their agents and private collectors for permission to reproduce photographs.

Both Caroline and I would like to thank the publication team – our eagle-eyed copy-editor Mark Sutcliffe, designer Christoph Stolberg and publishers Edward and Julia Booth-Clibborn who between them proved that miracles could happen.

Jane Pritchard

With Jack in the garden of Ivy House 1927

This publication was made possible with the generous support of:

Elena Heinz
The Linbury Trust
The Monument Trust
The Rothschild Foundation
Trusthouse Charitable Foundation

Proceeds from the sale of this book will go to the Royal Ballet School's Student Scholarship and Bursary Programme

The Royal Ballet School is recognised as one of the world's greatest ballet schools. Admission is based solely on artistic merit and potential and the School prides itself in never turning away a talented student due to lack of financial means. Around 96% of students rely on financial support to attend The Royal Ballet School and where this is not met by the Department for Education, students are supported by the School's Student Scholarship and Bursary programme. Approximately £600,000 has to be raised annually to ensure that any student possessing the talent to train at The Royal Ballet School, has the opportunity to do so. Registered Charity No: 214364

 THE ROYAL BALLET SCHOOL

www.royalballetschool.co.uk

Concept, Graphic Design: Christoph Stolberg
Editor: Mark Sutcliffe
Editorial assistance: Cecilia Grayson

First published in 2012 by Booth-Clibborn Editions in the United Kingdom
www.booth-clibborn.com

© text Jane Pritchard, Caroline Hamilton
© images (please refer to next page)

A cataloging-in-publication record for this book is available
from the publisher

ISBN 978-1-86154-335-6

Colour Separation: Bildpunkt GmbH, Berlin
Printed and bound in Italy by Castelli Bolis Poligrafiche S.p.A.

PICTURE CREDITS

Page 6. Portrait in Vienna, Ursula Hageli Collection

Page 8. Zulma in *Giselle* Act II, St Petersburg. Photography by Fischer, St Petersburg, 1899. Photograph Dorothy Gummer donation, Theatre & Performance Department, V&A © V&A Images

Page 11. Pavlova and Mikhail Fokine in *The Awakening of Flora* at the Maryinsky. Photograph Fischer, St Petersburg 1900, Theatre & Performance Department, V&A © V&A Images

Page 12. Pavlova as *Spanish Doll* in *The Fairy Doll.* Photograph Fischer, St Petersburg 1903

Page 13. Design by Léon Bakst for the Spanish Doll in *The Fairy Doll,* 1903

Page 14. Private class with Enrico Cecchetti in Pavlova's St Petersburg apartment *c.* 1909. Photograph 1998.023.0108, Performing Arts Collection, Arts Centre Melbourne

Page 16. *In Pharoah's Daughter,* Moscow. Photo by Fischer, Moscow, 1906, Theatre & Performance Department, V&A © V&A Images

Page 18. In *La Bayadère.* Photograph by Fischer St Petersburg 1903, Cyril W. Beaumont Collection Theatre & Performance Collections, V&A © V&A Images

Page 19. *Chopiniana.* Photograph Fischer, St Petersburg, 1907

Page 20. Pavlova in rehearsal dress © Museum of London

Page 22. In *La Fille mal gardée.* Photograph: Schneider, Berlin, 1909

Page 24. Cover of *Le Théâtre* May 1909 showing *Le Pavillon d'Armide,* Theatre & Performance Department, V&A © V&A Images

Page 26. *Giselle* 1910

Page 27. Poster for 1909 Saison Russe. Theatre & Performance Department, V&A © V&A Images

Page 28. Pavlova in *Bacchanale.* Photograph Schneider, Berlin

Page 30. At the door of Ivy House. Photograph Lafayette 1927

Pages 32/33. Pavlova in bay window of her dining room. Photograph Lafayette 1927

Page 34. Going up to the terrace soon after her acquisition of Ivy House. Photograph Press Association

Pages 36/37. With her swans and flamingos. Photograph Topical Press Agency 1930

Page 38. Posing by an urn in the garden at Ivy House. Photograph Daily Mirror

Page 40. With Dandré at the bottom of the Garden, © Museum of London

Page 41. Tea with Enrico Cecchetti in the garden 1927, Cyril W. Beaumont Collection, Theatre & Performance Department, V&A © V&A Images

Page 42. Playing croquet with Novikoff and Chaliapin Photograph Graphic Studio 1923. Cyril W. Beaumont Collection, Theatre & Performance Department, V&A © V&A Images

Page 43. Pavlova and pets 1912, © Museum of London

Pages 44 & 45. With pupils at Ivy House 1913, © Museum of London

Pages 46/47. Ivy House in 1931

Page 49. With tulips after she returned to Ivy House. Photograph Graphic Photo Union 1920, Theatre & Performance Department, V&A © V&A Images

Page 50. Pavlova in costume for *La Nuit.* Photograph Graphic Photo Union, Cyril W. Beaumont Collection, Theatre & Performance Department, V&A © V&A Images

Page 52. *Valse Caprice.* Photograph Dover Street 1910

Page 53. Evocation of *La Nuit*

Pages 54/55. *Russian Dance* in Ivy House Studio. Photograph Daily Mirror *c.* 1912, © Museum of London

Page 56. In costume for the *Russian Dance.* Photograph Foulsham and Banfield 1910

Page 57. Costume for the *Russian Dance.* Photograph © Museum of London

Pages 58/59. Pavlova and Mordkin in costume for the *Russian Dance.* Photograph Cyril W. Beaumont Collection, Theatre & Performance Department, V&A © V&A Images

Page 61. The Palace Theatre of Varieties 1911

Pages 62 & 63. Fliers for the Palace Theatre, London 1911 & 1912. Theatre & Performance Department, V&A © V&A Images

Page 64. *Columbine* on front of 1912 tour programme

Page 65. Design by Léon Bakst for *Oriental Fantasy* 1913, Theatre & Performance Department, V&A © V&A Images

Page 66. Pavlova and Novikoff in the *Bacchanale* Photograph Schneider, Berlin, 1913, Theatre & Performance Department, V&A © V&A Images

Page 67. Bleichmann pas de deux. Photograph Foulsham and Banfield 1910

Page 69. Curtain call at the London Opera House. Photograph Daily Mirror 1913, Helen Ordish Collection

Pages 70/71. Pavlova's company arrives at Liverpool in September 1912. Pavlova in the centre with lilies between Gashewska and Roshanara. Photograph Carbonarra 1912, Theatre & Performance Department, V&A © V&A Images

Page 72. *Amarilla.* Photograph Campbell Grey 1912, Theatre & Performance Department, V&A © V&A Images

Page 74. Costume for *Amarilla.* Photograph © Museum of London

Page 76. Costume design by Georges Barbier for *Amarilla*. 1919, Theatre & Performance Department, V&A © V&A Images

Page 77. *Amarilla*. Photograph Foulsham and Banfield, London, 1912

Page 78. Four costume designs by Georges Barbier for *Amarilla*. 1919, Theatre & Performance Department, V&A © V&A Images

Pages 80/81, 82, 83. *Amarilla*. Photographs Foulsham and Banfield, London, 1912, Theatre & Performance Department, V&A © V&A Images

Page 86. Studio portrait, photograph Schneider, Berlin 1909, Cyril W. Beaumont Collection Theatre & Performance Department, V&A © V&A Images

Page 87. *Above:* At her garden party at Ivy House 1912. Photograph Press Association
Below: Double page spread from *The Tatler,* 1913

Page 88. Fashion portraits

Page 89. *Right:* Leaving Ivy House for Waterloo Station. Photograph Daily Mail 1913, White Lodge Museum & Ballet Resource Centre
Left: In New York. Photograph by Mishkin 1917, Cyril W. Beaumont Collection, Theatre & Performance Department, V&A © V&A Images

Page 90. In a 'Delphos' gown by Fortuny 1914, White Lodge Museum & Ballet Resource Centre

Page 91. On the roofs in New York. Photographs Keystone and Topical Press 1923, © Museum of London

Page 92. *Right:* Eve magazine 1925. *Left:* Posing through the window of a third class train carriage October 1927, © Museum of London

Page 93. *Above:* By the lake at Ivy House. *Below:* Shoes by A. Argence, Paris, © Museum of London

Page 94. At Ivy House 1930 and in 1920s, Helen Ordish Collection

Page 95. *Left:* Selfridges window in tribute to Pavlova 1925. *Right:* Advertisements for Best and Co. from the programme for Manhattan Opera House in November 1924

Page 96. *Left:* Advertisement for Mercolised Wax from a programme for His Majesty's Theatre, Melbourne 1929. *Right:* Advertisement for Odol mouthwash from programme for London Coliseum 1910

Page 97. *Left:* Advertisement for Arthur Franks ballet shoes from the *Dancing Times* October 1921.
Right: Advertisement for Cantilever Shoes from *The Tatler* in 1927 and advertisement for Rayne's shoes from the 1925 Covent Garden programme.

Page 98. *Left:* Advertisements for Exquisite Silk Stockings from the programme for Manhattan Opera House in November 1924. *Right:* Advertisements for Welte-Mignon and Baldwin Pianos from American tour programme

Page 99. Pavlova in tailored suit, © Museum of London

Page 101. In Melbourne. Photograph Edwin G. Adamson, © Museum of London

Page 102. Anna Pavlova as the Fairy Doll by Joseph Rous Paget-Fredericks. White Lodge Museum & Ballet Resource Centre

Page 104. Anna Pavlova in costume for *The Fairy Doll* backstage at the Royal Opera House Photograph Abbé 1923, © Museum of London

Page 106. Rehearsal at Golders Green Hippodrome Topical Press, © Museum of London

Page 108. Anna Pavlova and Alexandre Volinine in *Autumn Leaves*. Photograph Abbé 1920

Page 109. Cartoon by Nerman from *the Tatler* 26 September 1923

Page 110. Aubrey Hitchens as the North Wind, Anna Pavlova as the *Chrysanthemum* and Vladimorov as the Poet in *Autumn Leaves* at the Alhambra Theatre, Glasgow. *Daily Record,* Glasgow November 1930

Page 113. *Above Left* and *below* in Don Quixote with Novikoff. Photograph Abbé 1924, © Museum of London. *Above Right Giselle* on stage at the Royal Opera House, *The Times,* Helen Ordish Collection

Pages 114/115. Pavlova's company posed on stage in *The Fairy Doll,* 1920s, © Museum of London

Page 117. *Above: Mexican Dance,* © Museum of London *Below:* with Algeranoff and company in *Oriental Impressions*

Pages 118/119. The company in Bremen 1930, © Museum of London

Page 120. Sequence of stills from *The Swan* from the *Illustrated London News*, 1936

Page 122. Pavlova with Mary Pickford. Photograph General Photographic Agency, 1925, © Museum of London

Page 123. *Californian Poppy*

Page 126. Fenella thrown into prison; a still from *The Dumb Girl of Portici,* © Museum of London

Page 127. Pavlova with her dressers on the set, 1915, © Museum of London

Page 128. Still from *The Dumb Girl of Portici*

Page 129. *Invitation to the Dance,* © Museum of London

Page 130. During the shooting of *The Dumb Girl of Portici,* London Archives of the Dance, Theatre & Performance Department, V&A © V&A images

Page 133. Edmund Nakhimoff, Algeranoff and corps de ballet filming for *The Immortal Swan,* 1935, © Museum of London

Page 135. 'Riverside Revel' at Kew. Photograph London News Agency, Cyril W. Beaumont Collection, Theatre & Performance Department, V&A © V&A Images

Page 137. Pavlova visiting the Laura Knight exhibition. Cyril W. Beaumont Collection, Theatre & Performance Department, V&A © V&A Images

Page 138. The original display of costumes and memorabilia at the Museum of London at Kensington Palace in the 1930s

Page 140. Exhibition at the Archives de la danse, Paris. Photograph Chevojon 1934

Page 142. Pavlova in *Christmas* in Berlin, 1924

Page 144. Programme cover for Matthew Bourne's *Swan Lake*, 1984

Page 145. With Jack in the garden of Ivy House. Photograph Lafayette 1927, Theatre & Performance Department, V&A ©V&A Images

Page 146. *Gavotte Pavlova*, photograph Andrew Studio, New Zealand 1926, Theatre & Performance Department, V&A ©V&A Images

Page 147. *The Dragonfly.* Photograph Hill Studios New York, Helen Ordish Collection

Page 148. *Above:* London Festival Ballet in Mary Skeaping's *Giselle*. Photograph © Alan Cunliffe 1971. *Below:* Margot Fonteyn in *Marguerite and Armand*. Photograph Anthony Crickmay, 1963, Theatre & Performance Department, V&A © V&A Images

Page 149. Ursula Hageli in costume for *Bacchanale*. Photograph © Don Chesser

Page 150. In her swan costume in the garden at Ivy House. Photograph Central News © Museum of London

Page 152. *The Swan.* Photograph Schneider, Berlin

Page 153 Costumes for *The Swan*, © Museum of London

Page 154. *The Swan*

Page 158. With Uday Shankar in *Krishna and Radha*

Page 162. Pavlova in Bombay. Photograph *Daily Mirror,* 1923, © Museum of London

Page 165. With Alexander Jacovleff at Salzo-Maggiore Photograph Moreschi Salzo-Maggiore, Cyril W. Beaumont Collection, Theatre & Performance Department, V&A © V&A Images

Page 166. On holiday at Salzo-Maggiore. Photograph Moreschi Salzo-Maggiore, Cyril W. Beaumont Collection, Theatre &Performance Department, V&A © V&A Images

Page 168. Pavlova preparing her shoes in her apartment in St Petersburg

Page 170. With Jack in the garden of Ivy House. Photograph Lafayette, 1927

Page 175. On holiday at Salzo-Maggiore. Photograph Moreschi Salzo-Maggiore, Cyril W. Beaumont Collection, Theatre & Performance Department, V&A © V&A Images

Endpapers. Details of newspaper clippings and other pictures of Pavlova mounted on folding screens by Frederick Ashton in the 1920s and 30s. He was obsessed with her and watched her dance whenever he could. She greatly influenced his work.
By kind permission of Julie Kavanagh and Ross MacGibbon. Photographed by Richard Davies

All uncredited photographs are from private collections.

In the 1920s Pavlova chose to holiday at Salzo-Maggiore in Northern Italy where she could relax,
take advantage of the spa, draw and sculpt